Child discipline. It's an issue that you, as a parent, will face time and again. Unfortunately, it's not quite as simple as vaccinations and shoe tying. The "old school" demands repression—which often fosters a future rebellion problem. Today's "experts" call for self-expression—and we see another "me" generation in the making. Most of us, however, fall somewhere in between. And, when frustration occasionally gets the better of our convictions, we shake our heads and say, "There must be a better way!"

Indeed, there is, asserts Larry Tomczak. It's positive, effective, and, most importantly of all, **God-ordained.** It's a scriptural approach whereby affection and correction go hand-in-hand. And its practical applications are yours in this unique handbook. Here is a truly biblical method to help you shape your children into the kind of people God—and you—want them to be.

God, the Rod, and Your Child's Bod

The Art of Loving Correction
for Christian Parents

Larry Tomczak

Fleming H. Revell Company
Old Tappan, New Jersey

Library of Congress Cataloging in Publication Data

Tomczak, Larry, date
God, the rod, and your child's bod.

Bibliography: p.
1. Discipline of children—Religious aspects—Christianity. I. Title.
HQ770.4.T65   649'.64   81-23507
ISBN 0-8007-5082-9   AACR2

Contents

A Jewish couple, Manoah and his wife, were childless. One day, an angel came to the woman and informed her she would have a son who would be used to deliver the nation of Israel from their persecutors, the Philistines. Upon hearing this word, Manoah immediately turned to God for guidance. "O, Lord, I pray thee, let the man of God whom thou didst send come again to us, and teach us what we are to do with the boy that will be born" (Judges 13:8).

God answered Manoah's prayer and the angel came again to tell Manoah and his wife how to rear their child, in preparation for his calling.

This couple began their parenting responsibility by acknowledging their lack of expertise and seeking God's direction. May I invite you to do likewise as you begin this book.

Remember, "God opposes the proud, but gives grace to the humble" (James 4:6). It's not that "God helps those who help themselves." God helps those who admit they *can't* help themselves.

Preface

"Why can't you act normal!"

Glaring at her five-year-old daughter while standing in the parking lot, the blond young mother was obviously upset.

"That's because she's *not* normal!" the dad injected. Gritting his teeth, he added, "Now get in this car."

Head lowered, the little girl stopped singing and complied.

The girl's offense? She had been skipping merrily alongside her parents on their way to the car. Whether the afternoon heat or the store's prices provoked the outburst was unclear. One thing *was* clear: the crushed spirit of a little child.

Retreating to the pancake house early Saturday morning, you sit down with your morning paper for a quiet "get away" breakfast. The stillness is abruptly shattered as Dad, Mom, and their "turbulent trio" park themselves alongside your table.

Splat.

There goes the ketchup bottle, inches from your foot, as the six-year-old elbows his way into the booth. A smack to the head is but the beginning of the drama to unfold.

The four-year-old in pigtails jabs her brother for grabbing one of her pancakes, and immediately receives a viselike grip to the knee.

"Ouch!"

There goes the milk. And here come Mom's daggers as she glares and hisses, "You're never coming with us again!"

As the two-year-old whines repeatedly for "hammaburg and frinch fries," Dad ignores her yet can't conceal the smoldering within. He downs his coffee and leaves frustrated Mom to handle the offenders.

Another smack . . . further threats . . . defiant looks . . . the beat goes on.

You sit vicariously exhausted during the half-hour fiasco and can't help but think, *There's got to be a better way.*

These incidents happened last week. They are repeated in one form or another all over the country. Sometimes a child is smacked. Other times he is verbally attacked. Yet children do disobey. They do get on one's nerves at times. And parents do need to do something. Don't we?

Today the majority of young couples receive little or no preparation for parenting. Many of them don't have fathers and mothers in the area to guide them. Others receive some input, but it is piecemeal at best.

In light of the pressures mounting against the family today, a practical handbook is needed.

Growing out of my experience and that of the church community of which I am a part, I submit this book for your reading. Based on the positive experience of thousands of people who have faithfully followed the principles outlined within, I can assure you success if you'll follow the instructions.

LARRY TOMCZAK

God, the Rod, and
Your Child's Bod

1

An Introduction to Loving Correction

Did you ever stop to think that Jesus had to be fed, changed, and potty trained? Even though He never married and raised children of His own, He does know what parenting is all about. Having been raised in a human family gave Him firsthand exposure to the same challenge moms and dads face today. Therefore, He can "sympathize with our weaknesses" and beckon us to "draw near to the throne of grace, that we may receive mercy and find grace to help in time of need" (Hebrews 4:15, 16).

Today is certainly a "time of need." Mounting pressures in our secular culture are assaulting the family and attempting to undermine its very existence. Supports in society which once undergirded the home are crumbling before our very eyes. Government institutions, mass media, and schools can no longer be relied upon to support Christian family life. Indeed, they often prove actively hostile. Just last evening as I listened to the national news on television, the newsman spoke of the "kitchen, children, church trap" of American women.

Many of us are aware that "times they are a changin'," but do we realize how serious and dramatic these changes really are? Recently *U.S. News & World Report* did a cover story on "The American Family" which began with a memo from the magazine's president. He stated: "We were all aware that there have been big changes in families, but the extent of those changes astounded us as we began to look into the situation."

Have you recently taken a look into the situation? Remember the frog that was placed in a pan of cold water on a stove. The heat was turned on so low that he did not even notice the change in temperature until it was too late. He was cooked.

Consider the following items which are indicative of current societal trends. Cataclysmic changes and social upheaval are all around us. Are we paying attention?

Traditional Family: Today a scant 13 percent of our nation's families include a working father, stay-at-home mother, and one or more children. In 1950, 18 percent of the nation's mothers worked outside the home. Today, for the first time in modern history, working wives outnumber housewives (51 percent). "Six million mothers with children under six are working, but how are they caring for seven million kids?" (*Newsweek* magazine).

Single Parents: Today, one in every five children lives in a single-parent household. Eighteen million children live in what was once called a "broken home." This figure is up 40 percent in only ten years! Fully 45 percent of the children born today may spend at least part of their childhood with only one parent. Comparing children from broken homes with those who live with both parents, the ratio for school dropouts is 9 to 5, and for expulsions 8 to 1.

Divorce: Divorce rates in the United States are now the highest in the world. Five out of every nine marriages (55 percent) end in divorce. (One hundred years ago the figure was one in every thirty-two.) Forty-seven states now have "no-fault" divorces to make it even easier to end a marriage. A California court now allows group divorce sessions where judges grind divorces out at a rate of thirty every two-and-a-half minutes. "Do it yourself" divorce kits are now available. At present, over 1 million children a year are involved in divorce cases.

The American Family: Only one household in three has a father, mother, and their natural children.

Anti-Family Feminist Forces:

> Marriage has existed for the benefit of men and has been a legally sanctioned method of control over women . . . the end of the institution of marriage is a necessary condition for the liberation of women. Therefore, it is important for us to encourage women to leave their husbands and not to live individually with men . . . we must work to destroy it [marriage].
>
> The Document, Declaration of Feminism

> For the sake of those who wish to live in equal partnership, we have to abolish and reform the institution of legal marriage.
>
> Gloria Steinem, editor of *Ms.* magazine

No deity will save us, we must save ourselves. Promises of immortal salvation or fear of eternal damnation are

both illusory and harmful.
Humanist Manifesto II, signed by Betty Friedan, foun-
der of National Organization for Women (N.O.W.)

Living Together: Once considered immoral and illegal,
rough estimates tell us over 3 million men and women
live together unmarried. Magazines, newspapers, movies,
and television regularly feature actors, actresses, music
celebrities, and sports heroes (those children tend to
emulate) in such a live-in arrangement. "In 1957, 80 percent of those questioned said unwed people who live together were immoral. In 1976, only 25 percent gave negative responses on the subject" (Institute of Social
Research, University of Michigan).

Teenagers: Teenage pregnancies have increased by 33
percent in the past five years. Recently there were 1.1
million teen pregnancies. Three out of every four were
illegitimate. Of the total, 554,000 ended in births and
434,000 in abortions. Venereal disease is beyond epi-
demic proportions. According to the latest survey by B.
Dalton bookstores, an author whose writing highlights
immoral sexual conduct holds three of the top five sellers
in juvenile books. Teen literature today is certainly a far
cry from *Little Women* and *Mutiny on the Bounty.*

Abortion: Today, a doctor has to have parental permis-
sion to give a teenager a tonsillectomy, but not an abortion. Most people are vaguely aware that on the average
one unborn child is legally extinguished every thirty seconds, hour upon hour, day after day. Since the Supreme

Court decision of 1973, the number of deaths has totaled seven times those of the revolutionary war, the Civil War, World War I, World War II, the Korean War, and the Vietnam War combined. Since 1973, more than 9 million babies have been murdered. Presently being developed is "Prostoglandin"—a do-it-yourself abortion suppository, shifting abortion from hospitals and clinics to one's own bathroom. (A car recently seen had two bumper stickers on it: SAVE THE SEALS and KEEP ABORTION SAFE AND LEGAL.)

Child Abuse: A national problem, with over 2 million battered-child cases yearly. This causes more deaths than any single childhood disease. In our own county in Maryland, twenty-five people work full time on child-abuse cases.

Drugs: Increased usage among youth is exceptionally dramatic. Since 1962, the proportion of youth (eighteen to twenty-six) who have tried marijuana has jumped from 4 percent to almost 70 percent. Those who have taken harder drugs—including cocaine, heroin, and angel dust—has risen from 3 percent to 33 percent. Rock music and youth-oriented movies glamorize drugs and push for marijuana legalization. (Forty-one scientists from fourteen nations recently presented papers showing the dangerous effects of marijuana on the brain, lungs, and reproductive organs. Smoking 3 to 5 joints a week is the equivalent of 112 tobacco cigarettes.)

Television and Movies: Today the average adult spends more than 44 hours weekly (6.2 hours daily) in front of the TV. Children average 54 hours per week. By high-school graduation, teens will have logged at least 15,000 hours (more than any other activity except sleep). Television is now rated the most powerful influence in American life. Programming featuring adultery, fornication, violence, homosexuality, nudity, and anti-family themes are commonplace. With video cassettes, cable, and pay TV, the technological wave of the 80s, sexually explicit film sales are booming. Many campuses now hold a student-sponsored "Erotic Week" featuring porno films such as *Deep Throat* and *The Devil in Miss Jones.* Recently, New York's highest court cut the heart of the state's "kiddie porn" law. Citing free-speech rights, it overturned the conviction of a man who sold films involving naked children performing sexual acts.

Today's soap operas have a new brazenness as well. According to a Michigan State study, researchers discovered that nearly 80 percent of the scenes in which intercourse was suggested occurred between unmarried lovers—and only 6 percent involved married partners. The highest-rated daytime show, with 14 million daily viewers, was found to contain the most sexual activity.

Schools: Newsweek magazine recently did a cover story, "Why Public Schools Fail." From the report came the following:

In a *Newsweek*-Gallup Poll, nearly half the respondents say schools are doing a poor or only fair job—a verdict that would have been unthinkable just seven years ago, when two-thirds in a similar poll rated schools excellent or good. A poll last year by the National Education Association showed that 41 percent of all teachers regretted having become teachers in the first place. What is the single most important problem facing public schools today? *Lack of discipline.*

(The report also cited that while public-school enrollment is dwindling every year and more and more public schools are closing, on the average, three new Christian schools are opening daily!)

In the most recent *People* magazine nationwide readers' poll, the question was asked: "Are American kids getting out of control?"

The response: " 'And how,' sigh seven out of ten readers, most of them weary parents and grandparents."

The family in this country is in serious trouble, yet it is absolutely critical to the survival of a nation. This is why I believe, with the growing darkness coming upon the world, that God is speaking a word about preparation for "perilous times" (2 Timothy 3:1–5 KJV). He is emphasizing three essentials for the Christian family to flourish in a hostile society:

1. *Authority of the Word of God.* In a humanistic society, the holy Scriptures (not opinion polls or noted authorities) must retain their preeminent position as our guide for every facet of life.
2. *Active relationship with the Lord Jesus Christ.* Successful parenting entails more than simply acquiring a set of

techniques. It's not enough to know biblical principles; one must be vitally and uncompromisingly related to the Person who enables us to walk in them.

3. *Authentic commitment in a Christian fellowship.* The family is not meant to exist as an island in a sea of separatism but as a life-giving organism within the supportive environment of authentic Christian community (not merely a meeting to attend but a life-style to be lived).

Running parallel to the disintegration of the family in society is the restoration of the family in the Christian church. God's plan is to have "biblical showcase examples" to provoke mankind to jealousy and thereby draw them into His glorious end-time purpose.

"A prudent man foresees the difficulties ahead and prepares for them; the simpleton goes blindly on and suffers the consequences" (Proverbs 22:3 TLB).

One aspect of family life which is under attack today is that of child discipline or, as I call it, loving correction. No subject is more misunderstood. Yet few things are so essential to the establishment and maintenance of healthy, stable family life. Let's examine loving correction: what it is, who is responsible, and what are its basic elements. *God, the Rod, and Your Child's Bod* may seem like an amusing title, but it is only a lead-in to a subject which is truly serious business.

> But whoever causes one of these little ones who believe in me to sin, it would be better for him to have a great millstone fastened round his neck and to be drowned in the depth of the sea.
>
> Matthew 18:6

A bumper sticker often seen reads: INSANITY IS IN-HERITED. YOU GET IT FROM YOUR CHILDREN. Let us rather embrace the truth that appears on a plaque hanging in our home:

IT IS BETTER TO BUILD CHILDREN THAN TO REPAIR MEN.

2

What Is It?

Satan is an extremist. He distorts what God ordains. He then parades it as a counterfeit to deceive others from seeing the authentic. Yet the counterfeit always ensures the existence of the real.

Did you know that when the F.B.I. trains its agents to recognize counterfeit bills, it has them spend hour upon hour examining the real thing? The reason is simple: A person so familiarized with the authentic has no trouble identifying the counterfeit.

Over the years, many distortions and misconceptions have arisen concerning correction of children. As a result, some have "thrown the baby out with the bath water" by rejecting what they think is biblical correction. Others have "drunk the dirty bath water" by accepting distortions, not knowing what else to do.

Someone recently remarked, "Everything in the modern home is controlled by a switch except the children!"

Recently, *Parents* magazine ran an article entitled, "Confessions of a Non-Spanker." The author of the article attempted to convey that her son was much better off since she "kicked the spanking habit" (something she compared with "giving up smoking"). A careful reading of the article revealed the type of correction she "kicked" was a counterfeit of the real. So, too, was her response to her child's misbehavior.

> I started yelling. Really frothing at the mouth. I stopped my hand inches from his face. I . . . realized the screaming shrew who had almost slapped her tiny son in the face. . . . I have faced the fact that handling my own anger by screaming myself hoarse and slapping . . . does not teach my child self-control or discipline. I'm polite to him and respect his rights and dignity.

As sincere as the author may be, the kind of correction she stopped has nothing to do with authentic biblical correction.

Our challenge is to become so familiar with genuine child correction according to the Word of God that we are never again hoodwinked by unbiblical extremes.

Two unbiblical extremes of loving correction are the *disciplinarian* and *libertarian* approaches.

The disciplinarian approach is an overreaction to balanced discipline. It is militaristic. Cold. Stern. Catchphrases like the following may be heard: "Spare the rod and spoil the child." "Children should be seen, not heard." "Do as I say, not as I do." "If you don't like it, there's the door." The rod or hand is quickly used by an angry parent for anything, anytime, anywhere. If no rod or hairbrush is available, a slap across the face or smack to the head will do. Usually the blowup stems from fatigue and/or frustration and often ends with, "Now get to your room!" (NOTE: Reports of child abuse spring from this approach carried to its extreme, not from loving correction applied in the spirit of Christ.)

Many of us grew up with some form of the disciplinarian approach to correction, and hence we recoil whenever we hear terms like *child discipline* or *the rod.* Besides, we recall those rat-maze studies in school which "proved" that punishment doesn't really influence human behavior. Noted child psychologists have given us a more sophisticated way to bring up our children in the twentieth century.

The libertarian approach stresses the inherent goodness of the child. Never repress. Never frustrate. Allow the child to express his feelings honestly and openly. Temper tantrums will be outgrown if ignored. Never spank a child, for it inhibits growth, bruises the ego, threatens security, and contributes to violence in society. Spanking is an assault on the dignity of a child. It is dehumanizing. Give rewards and incentives but never impose your values upon him. Let him develop naturally into his full personhood.

Last week I was finishing up some grocery shopping when, upon leaving the checkout line, I saw a freckled two-year-old begin to assert himself. Beneath his I'M GRANDMA'S BOY tee shirt was a superstrong self-will.

"Come here, please. It's time to go," beckoned the young, tanned mommy.

"No," junior defied, adjusting his Yankee cap firmly in place.

"Oh, come on," she coaxed.

Throwing himself down on the tiled floor, he cranked up the tears, stomped his feet, and made sure she knew he wasn't budging.

Gritting her teeth, she stiffened her torso, spun around, and walked out of the store.

As she vanished from sight, the toddler (whose outburst was now at the wailing stage) jumped up and ran, terrified, after his disappearing mom. I ran right behind him lest he dart into the stream of oncoming cars beyond the exit doors. Turning the corner, his mother picked him up like a sack of charcoal and steamed off to the car. Feet flying, arms waving, head jerking, "Grandma's boy" continued to "express his feelings honestly and openly" while "developing naturally into his full personhood."

In the Bible is a verse which comes to mind: "Claiming to be wise, they became fools" (Romans 1:22).

Both of these approaches are counterfeits and extremes. Everywhere people are realizing that yesterday's permissive parental attitudes have produced the rebellion evidenced in the younger generation today. Moreover, many of us are victims of our own parents' style of discipline (although many did the best they could, having only what was passed on to them).

On certain products you'll find the label: "For best results follow the instructions of the manufacturer." And for best results in marriage and rearing children, we must follow the instructions of the One who created us and ordained the family unit.

Whether His instructions please our intellect or emotions is beside the point. We must move ahead in obedience and faith (not an "Okay, I'll try it and see if it works" attitude). *All progress in the Christian life is by faith.* "And without faith it is impossible to please him [God]" (Hebrews 11:6).

"All scripture is inspired by God and profitable for teaching, for reproof, for correction, and for training in righteousness" (2 Timothy 3:16).

Notice the words *correction* and *training in righteousness.* The Lord wouldn't have put them there if there wasn't a need for them.

Loving correction is the biblical procedure for training children in righteousness so that they will become self-disciplined individuals. It is educating a child and overseeing his choices in an atmosphere of unconditional love, until he can make wise choices of his own. In doing so, we help him become self-disciplined. "Listen to counsel and accept discipline, That you may be wise the rest of your days" (Proverbs 19:20 NAS).

The primary goal of loving correction is to produce godly character in our children so that God will be glorified. Our goal is not merely to find a little peace in troubled times at home. We are participating in shaping lives so that our children's character will reflect God's glory (His manifest presence) for all eternity.

Loving correction (child discipline) means far more than punishing. Punishment is what you do *to* a child. Discipline is what you do *for* a child. Punishment, a part of loving correction, is derived from a Latin word meaning "pain." It is inflicting pain on a person for misbehavior.

Discipline comes from the same root as *disciple,* meaning "to learn." In rearing children, we want them to *learn* self-control; in other words, initial parental control gives way to self-control. The Bible speaks of a father who "manages his own household well, keeping his children under control . . ." (1 Timothy 3:4 NAS). If God says so, He must know that children have a need to be controlled.

Scripture not only teaches corporal punishment for disobedience and wrong attitudes in children but it commands it as well. *Consistent correction is not an elective but a directive from Almighty God.* Unless you establish this fact in your heart, you'll be tempted—when it's inconvenient (you're on the phone, in a supermarket, or eating dinner) or when such thoughts arise as "My child is different" . . . "It's probably too late"—to compromise or "cop out." But let us emphasize this right from the onset: *The rod of correction will only bring true success when administered in the context of a strong, healthy, love bond between parents and child.*

Now let's examine what God's Word says about loving correction.

"Foolishness is bound in the heart of a child; but the rod of correction shall drive it far from him" (Proverbs 22:15 KJV).

Contrary to modern, humanistic thinking concerning the "inherent goodness of a child," the Bible makes it clear that "foolishness" (literal Hebrew, "waywardness") is bound up in a child's heart (the center of his being). No one has to teach him to be selfish, to lie, steal, or disobey; yet one must teach him to share, be honest, truthful, kind, and obedient. "His royal majesty, the baby," has a self-centered nature regardless of how cute and innocent he may look.

The word *foolishness* comes from "fool," and Psalms 14:1 says, "The fool says in his heart, 'There is no God.' " Or to paraphrase it, "I'll run my own life . . . do my own thing . . . be my own God." So Scripture says that when (not if) a child manifests this attitude of self-will, the rod of correction is applied to "drive it far from him." Remove the *nt* from parent and you get "pare" which means to remove or cut away.

In writing a book like this, it was important for me to remind myself of my children's foolish bent. That way I wouldn't have to feel as though my family must maintain some sort of image of perfection. My children do disobey—often! Yet of one thing you can be sure: I'll deal with such disobedience biblically, and sooner or later see the fruit. The mistakes I've made have been many, but I pray my experiences will now benefit you.

When my wife, Doris, and I teach a twelve-week course called "Creating a Successful Christian Home" in the fellowships in which we are building, we make sure a certain statement is made: "Don't freak out when you see our children disobey or display bad attitudes. They will. We guarantee it. Foolishness is bound up in their hearts. Do freak out, though, if we don't do anything about it. In fact, if we are negligent, please love us enough to alert us to our failure. Scripture says, 'Faithful are the wounds of a friend . . .' " (Proverbs 27:6).

"But won't this kind of correction drive my child away from me and repress his little personality?"

To such a fear the Scriptures respond in this fashion: "Train up a child in the way he should go, and when he is old [Hebrew: "has hair on his chin," that is to say, when he's approaching maturity, not when he's sixty] he will not depart from it" (Proverbs 22:6). The passage doesn't say, "he will depart and come back"; it says, "he will *not* depart from it."

Larry Christenson, well-known speaker and writer on the Christian family, observes that in the Bethany Fellowship in Minneapolis, the second generation (the people who grew up from childhood in that church community) is now involved in the leadership positions in the group. He states that almost without exception the second generation married and remained in the community, and this because no other life-style appealed to them.

This verse in Proverbs 22:6 directs us to "train up a child." "Train up" comes from the root word meaning "to develop a thirst, create a desire." This Old Testament term referred to the action of a Hebrew midwife dipping her finger into crushed dates and then rubbing the substance on the roof of a newborn mouth to stimulate sucking. In other words, parents are to live their lives in such a way as to develop a thirst in their children for their life-style. The rod is used to drive something out and our lives are used to draw someone in.

"Train up a child in the way he should go," and go that way yourself!

My favorite definition of the Christian family is "that place where parents so live the Christian life and so practice the presence of Christ that the children grow up to naturally accept God as the most important fact in life." As the classic poem says:

Children Learn What They Live

If a child lives with criticism, he learns to condemn.
If a child lives with hostility, he learns to fight.
If a child lives with ridicule, he learns to be shy.
If a child lives with shame, he learns to feel guilty.
If a child lives with tolerance, he learns to be patient.
If a child lives with encouragement, he learns
    confidence.
If a child lives with praise, he learns to appreciate.
If a child lives with fairness, he learns justice.
If a child lives with security, he learns to have faith.
If a child lives with approval, he learns to like himself.
If a child lives with acceptance and friendship, he learns
    to find love in the world.

DOROTHY LAW NOLTE

Let us turn now to the matter of repressing a child's personality.

In the verse which is before us ("Train up a child in the way he should go, and when he is old he will not depart from it") the words *in the way he should go* literally mean "in keeping with his individual bent" (that is, his nature as well as his unique set of personality characteristics). The Amplified Bible records it this way: "Train up a child in the way he should go [and in keeping with his individual gift or bent] . . . ." This means that every child brings with him into the world a specific nature—which the Bible calls "sinful" or selfish—as well as a set of unique, sealed orders from God. We are responsible to assist the child in curbing his selfish nature as well as to work with him to discover, develop, and deploy his gifts for the glory of God (Psalms 139:13–16).

In one sense, Proverbs 22:6 is not so much a promise as it is a warning to parents. In the Hebrew text, the phrase "in the way he should go" is actually missing. It reads instead, "Train up a child *in his way* and when he is old he will not depart from it." If you train up a child in *his* way—if you allow him to "do his thing" and develop the habit of self-expression in his youth—he'll not change when he's older. So let your child decide what he will and won't do, will and won't eat, will and won't wear, and God declares that that child will carry this undisciplined habit pattern right on into his future. Now that's a sobering warning. Jay Adams has put it this way in his book *Competent to Counsel:*

> The verse stands not as a promise but as a warning to parents that if they allow a child to train himself after his own wishes (permissively) they should not expect him to want to change these patterns when he matures. Children are born sinners and when allowed to follow their own wishes they will naturally develop sinful habit re-

sponses. The basic thought is that such habit patterns become deep-seated when they have been ingrained in the child from the earliest days. The corollary to this passage is found in Proverbs 19:18 where the writer exhorts the reader, "Discipline your son while there is hope; do not set your heart on his destruction."

Therefore, the two major bents we need to be aware of are the *evil bent*—the selfish self-will that needs to be curbed—and the *good bent*—the set of unique characteristics that need to be developed.

Let us also keep in mind that every child is different. This is why we shouldn't compare one child with another. One is more compliant, the other more defiant. One requires more work because he's determined (strong willed), and another requires less because she's docile (little girls can be strong willed, too!). Dr. James Dobson describes this in *The Strong-Willed Child:*

Just as surely as some children are naturally compliant, however, there are others who seem to be looking for a fight upon exit from the womb. Such a child comes into the world smoking a cigar and yelling about the temperature in the delivery room and the incompetence of the nursing staff. He expects meals to be served the instant they are ordered, and he demands every moment of his mother's time. As the months unfold, his expression of willful defiance becomes even more apparent, reaching a hurricane force during toddlerhood. This assertive little fellow is a precious human being who needs a special kind of understanding and discipline by his parents.

This should cause us to celebrate the wisdom of our God! Knowing this, we can cooperate with our Creator to release, not repress, our children's full potential.

"But," you may ask, "in rearing children, can't words, reproof, even scoldings get the job done? Can't these make my child wise? I know people who were brought up like this in the past and they seem to have turned out all right."

The biblical answer is: "By mere words a servant is not disciplined, for though he understands, he will not give heed" (Proverbs 29:19).

Yelling or simply commanding the child to go sit in the bedroom is unacceptable for it "gives opportunity to the devil" to sow bitterness and resentment as well as allowing guilt to fester without any quick release. Bribing is also off the mark in that it encourages a selfish attitude of "What's in it for me?" rather than a Christlike attitude of unselfish giving.

In addition, one must not lose sight of the day and age we're living in. Even one generation ago, our society provided many supports which fostered family life. Today, however, most of these supports are gone and society's attitudes toward marriage, sexuality, respect for authority, and family life have shifted in directions totally opposed to Christian principles. Drugs, abortion, homosexuality, and pornography, added to public acceptance of divorce, adultery, and premarital sex promoted by television, films, and music, all combine to produce an enormous challenge to families today. Without a total commitment to Christ, to His Word, and to a community of supportive believers, families are just not going to make it. I share this not to be dramatic, but to jolt those who need it into a sober realization of the urgency of the hour.

"But what if I raise my voice and show by my anger that I mean business about demanding obedience?" Note what the Bible has to say: "The anger of man does not work the righteousness of God" (James 1:20).

"But I love him too much! I don't want to lose his love. Besides, I heard Dr. Benjamin Spock, the child 'expert,' say, 'I don't think spanking is necessary.' "

We need to hear again what the Scriptures tell us: "Cease, my son, to hear the instruction that causeth to err from the words of knowledge" (Proverbs 19:27 KJV). "He who spares the rod hates his son, but he who loves him is diligent to discipline him" (Proverbs 13:24).

God's Word states that to *not* lovingly correct children is to hate them. To choose to withhold the brief moment of pain needed for correction which, by so doing, allows children to continue on in habit patterns which will eventually harm them, is not genuine love. It is misdirected, selfish "love." ("I've always given him everything he's ever wanted and I've never had to spank him. I don't like that approach. I don't like to see a child hurt. I . . . I . . . I. . . .")

Love, according to the Bible, is not mere sentiment or emotion. It is a costly commitment for the greatest good of another. *If you permit a child to nurture a habit which he will one day be forced (with greater difficulty) to break, you are the cruelest of parents.*

Today, some child "experts" say it's better to simply

leave the child to himself; let him grow up naturally to be free and uninhibited.

Yet in reality, isn't that what child abuse really is? Because some parents don't want to hurt their children, they disobey God, withhold loving correction, and thereby allow their children to continue down pathways to inevitable destruction and even eternal damnation. "Withhold not correction from the child: for if thou beatest [spank] him with the rod, he shall not die. Thou shalt beat [spank] him with the rod, and shalt deliver his soul from hell" (Proverbs 23:13, 14 KJV).

The biblical definition of the rod is a small, flexible branch from a tree (a wooden stick). Obviously, a child "shall not die" from a thin, wooden stick applied in love and control.

"The rod and reproof give wisdom, but a child left to himself brings shame to his mother" (Proverbs 29:15).

Yet some will ask, "Doesn't use of the rod contribute to violence in our society?"

The Bible teaches that the result of proper biblical discipline is "the peaceful fruit of righteousness" (Hebrews 12:11). Children know the difference between an objective spanking ministered in love and a beating springing from hostility and anger. God's Word assures us that the fruit or result of loving, parental discipline is peaceful self-control.

I contend that it is unfair to blame the violence in our society on the efforts of loving parents who are trying to raise their children scripturally by using the rod of correction to deal with behavior detrimental to their children, other people, and ultimately the children's relationship with God. Is not much of our present violence—rape, murder, assassination—actually a result of not having unacceptable behavior checked earlier in life through loving correction? Is not much of it really due to sex-and-violence-saturated television, wherein the average child in America today will have watched approximately sixteen thousand murders by the time he's sixteen? If we're going to talk about violence in our society, let's be brutally honest in diagnosing the real problem.

A recent article in our local paper stated:

> A 13-year-old boy is being held for the Russian roulette slaying of a neighborhood youngster in an incident police say took place in a reenactment of scenes from the Vietnam movie "The Deer Hunter." Officials ordered Gary B. held for the shooting death of John T., 8, killed last week while the two copied the Russian roulette scene from the film. The movie was aired on television several days before the incident.

In my files I have scores of articles exactly like the one above. The impact of sex-and-violence-saturated television cannot be ignored. Maybe a sticker should be attached to each TV set sold: "Warning: It has been determined that use of this product is hazardous to your spiritual and psychological health."

Everything you always wanted to know about how important television is in everyday American life can be answered with one single set of numbers: 97.9 percent of all American households have a television set. Only 96.8

percent of all American households have indoor plumbing!

It is nearly impossible to overstate the influence of television on America's family life.

But what about the pain and the crying associated with discipline? Several passages from the Bible address this very point: "Chasten thy son while there is hope, and let not thy soul spare for his crying" (Proverbs 19:18 KJV). "Blows that wound cleanse away evil; strokes make clean the innermost parts" (Proverbs 20:30). "Before I was afflicted I went astray; but now I keep thy word" (Psalms 119:67). "It is good for a man that he bear the yoke in his youth" (Lamentations 3:27).

Loving correction may not be pleasant or easy, but it is God's ordained way of training children, and He guarantees our success in writing: "For the moment all discipline seems painful rather than pleasant; later it yields the peaceful fruit of righteousness to those who have been trained by it" (Hebrews 12:11). (The Greek word here for training is *gumnazō,* from which we get our English word *gymnastics.* In other words, it means practicing something until it becomes natural.) "Correct thy son, and he shall give thee rest; yea, he shall give delight unto thy soul" (Proverbs 29:17 KJV).

"Peaceful fruit" . . . "rest" . . . "delight unto thy soul." Considering the grief and bitterness experienced by scores of parents at dinner tables and in supermarkets, the benefits are worth the investment.

"A foolish son is a grief to his father and bitterness to her who bore him" (Proverbs 17:25).

"But I still find it difficult. Why?"

The problem is that so many of us have never associated correction with love. In Hebrews 12:6, God declares, "For the Lord disciplines him whom he loves [these words, in fact, are inscribed on one of the rods in my home], and chastises every son whom he receives." And God should know; He had a Son whom it pleased Him to bruise (*see* Isaiah 53:10).

"Then I will punish their transgression with the rod and their iniquity with scourges" (Psalms 89:32).

Keep in mind that we are talking about correction, not rejection. Loving correction is never intended to humiliate or embarrass. It is never an excuse to be cruel, harsh, or oppressive. "As a father pities (Greek: "fondles") his children, so the Lord pities those who fear him" (Psalms 103:13), is the tenderness of spirit intended in carrying out biblical correction. A child is perceptive and can identify the difference between parental hostility and parental correction. A child should be taught to respond to "no" or a directive *in a normal voice,* and if he deliberately disobeys or displays a wrong attitude (pouting, whining, stomping feet, or slamming doors), he receives the "board of education on the seat of learning." (What follows this correction is most important and will be covered later.) When a child is very small (six to twenty months), raising your voice somewhat (not yelling) will probably be necessary at times. Be released to do so. Your motive is not one of anger and vengeance so much as it is to arrest the child's attention and make an impression. Saying a child's full name can also be helpful: "Justin

Mark, come here." Or repeat the first name twice as Jesus did: "Martha, Martha" (Luke 10:41), or "Saul, Saul" (Acts 9:4).

Loving correction reinforces with a painful experience the principle of the parents' authority over the child, and lets the child know that the particular action or attitude is unacceptable. He is totally secure in his parents' love.

Our heavenly Father "prunes" (removes what is unnecessary) "every branch" that "bears no fruit" (John 15:2). So, too, parents are given a tool by God "to remove or cut away": it's the rod of correction, not the rod of vengeance. Nor is it a magic wand to be applied in some mechanical way. It cannot be divorced from the context of a strong, healthy love bond between parents and child.

"And what if I 'blow it'; administer a spanking and later discover the child was sick or teething?"

First, nothing in our life should so challenge us to cry out for the grace and wisdom of God as the raising of our children. We must walk in a moment-by-moment dependency upon Him every day. In every difficult situation we should place a quick "phone call to glory" asking the Lord for His wisdom.

> If any of you lacks wisdom, let him ask God, who gives to all men generously and without reproaching, and it will be given him. But let him ask in faith, with no doubting, for he who doubts is like a wave of the sea that is driven and tossed by the wind. For that person must not suppose that a double-minded man, unstable in all his ways, will receive anything from the Lord.
>
> James 1:5–8

Second, we must always discern between willful disobedience and childishness. The Bible does say, "When I was a child . . . I reasoned like a child . . ." (1 Corinthians 13:11). Children are children, not full-fledged adults. They will accidently spill milk, act goofy, forget to do something, and so on. Here's where our understanding and tolerance comes in. Remember, in loving correction of our children we are talking of dealing with *discerned rebellion,* not crying due to gas, sickness, hunger, or discomfort.

Third, if you apply the rod in error, don't erect a monument to your mistake and sit for three days wallowing in guilt and condemnation. Simply ask the child's forgiveness and be assured that children are not as fragile as many of us think. They're flexible. They're tough. Plus, they forget quickly!

For best results, we are told, we should follow the instructions of the Manufacturer. "The rod has been shown to be an effective disobedience preventative device when used in a conscientiously applied program of oral affirmation and regular parental loving care."

Review

1. What are three essentials necessary for the Christian family to flourish in a hostile society? Why?
2. Name the two unbiblical extremes of loving correction. Explain them.
3. Define *loving correction.*

4. What is meant by "foolishness" in the heart of a child?
5. Explain fully the meaning of Proverbs 22:6, "Train up a child. . . ."
6. Respond to the accusation, "Loving correction is child abuse and contributes to violence in our society."
7. Are love and correction opposed to each other?

Response

Do I train my children by ignoring, punishing, or correction?

3

Who Is Responsible?

In the Bible there are descriptions of what happens when God allows judgment or a curse to befall a people who have abandoned His Word. Judgment is not always fire and brimstone falling or locusts biting people's legs!

> And I will make boys their princes, and babes shall rule over them. And the people will oppress one another, every man his fellow and every man his neighbor; the youth will be insolent to the elder. . . . When a man takes hold of his brother in the house of his father, saying: "You have a mantle; you shall be our leader . . ." in that day he will speak out, saying: "I will not be a healer; in my house there is neither bread nor mantle; you shall not make me leader of the people." . . . My people— children are their oppressors, and women rule over them. . . .
>
> Isaiah 3:4–7, 12

Reread the above passage and see if you can detect the curse coming upon our country as we are abandoning our Judeo-Christian foundations. Note the home in disarray; the leadership vacuum as men abdicate their responsibility; the emergence of dominant women in matriarchal

53

leadership; the rebellion of children and youth. Men today are called "male chauvinists," women "mindless robots," and parents "child abusers" if they adhere to biblical principles for the home.

The next chapter continues the curse:

> And seven women shall take hold of one man in that day, saying, "We will eat our own bread and wear our own clothes, only let us be called by your name; take away our reproach."
>
> Isaiah 4:1

In other words, independent mothers forsake their primary responsibility in the home ("keepers at home" [Titus 2:5 KJV] or those who "guide the house" [1 Timothy 5:14 KJV]). Unwilling to lower their standard of living to improve their quality of life, they seek out fulfillment working elsewhere in order to buy their food and clothing. (There are valid exceptions.) Men are necessary only to take away the reproach of being single and "unwanted." Society views as acceptable women being divorced and remarried as many as seven times. Flimsy excuses are put forth: "It was simply a bad marriage from the start".... "We found we were no longer compatible".... "I need to be able to grow as a person."

In the King James Version of Deuteronomy 28:41, we find another curse which God warned would come as an inevitable result of rejecting His Word: "Thou shalt beget sons and daughters, but thou shalt not enjoy them; for they shall go into captivity."

Has this not happened to millions of young people in

our Western civilization? They've "gone into captivity" to drugs, illicit sex, ungodly music, false religions, and countless other snares of Satan. As a result, their parents are unable to "enjoy them."

The United States population is now over 220 million. The United States Census revealed over 50 percent or over 110 million Americans are under twenty-five years of age. Consider: Over 1 million United States abortions per year—the majority are young people. Over 1 million runaways each year—the majority are young people. Over 1.5 million suicides each year (the number-two cause of death under the age of twenty-five)—the majority are young people. Over half a million junkies—the majority are young people. The "Moonies" boast of half a million followers—the majority are young people. T.M. (Transcendental Meditation) has 3 million adherents in the United States—the majority are young people. Homosexuals cite statistics of over 10 million in America—the majority are young people.

As never before in history, God is calling upon us to awaken to the seriousness of the hour and the significance of the home as the primary influence in shaping the destiny of lives. He is blowing an urgent trumpet for men to rise up and spearhead the way.

Realizing the significance of the home as the primary influence in shaping the destiny of lives, let's look at a few illustrations.

One of the main reasons teenage girls become promiscuous is a lack of affection from their fathers. To compensate, many get physically involved with young men as a means of security and gratification of the need for affection in their lives.

Why is it that millions of adult men find it extremely difficult to admit to their wives and children that they were wrong? One reason is that as young boys their dads were negative role models who would never admit they were wrong.

When parents ask, "What makes a happy child?" the answer is almost frightening in its import, for it must be, "We do!" The tie between parents and child is so close. A sampling of students were asked to rank factors which brought them the greatest happiness as children. "Happiness of parents" rated highest as a cause of happiness, while "parents quarreling" rated second only after "death or illness in the family" as the cause of greatest unhappiness.

Steven Judy, who recently was executed in Indiana for raping and strangling a young mother and then drowning her three children, aged five, four, and two, gave an interview prior to his death. His life was a trail of arrests for beatings, assaults, and rapes. A newspaper clipping featuring the interview went like this:

The oldest of four children in a broken family, Judy grew up in a poor, working class neighborhood in Indianapolis' South Side.

His father, Vernon, was arrested numerous times for beating his mother, Myrtle. Vernon Judy, a convicted felon, is a fugitive who escaped in 1971 from a work release program while serving a two- to fourteen-year sentence on a charge of conspiracy to defraud an insurance company.

During his murder trial, Judy testified that his father once butchered the family sheep dog after finding his mother in bed with another man.

Judy told reporters Friday, "As a child, if I had been raised by better parents or [had] some type of counseling when I was younger, I probably could have been different."

Lynette Fromme, the Manson follower convicted of attempting to assassinate Gerald Ford, said she was sitting on a curb in Venice, California, when Charles Manson approached her. She was lonely. Why did she follow? In her own words: "A beaten dog will follow anyone who loves it."

Gladys was a beautiful woman whose husband had deserted her. Edward was a tall Norwegian who left his wife and three children and lusted for fast motorcycles. They lived in adultery until Gladys became pregnant, and then Ed just split. Years later he was killed in a motorcycle accident, never having seen the little girl he had rejected along with her mother. The girl's name? Marilyn Monroe. Her life? Alcohol. Divorces. Nervous breakdown. Drug addiction. Finally suicide.

John Hinkley, Jr., the attempted assassin of Ronald Reagan, wandered aimlessly across this country. Who financed his wanderings? Apparently his wealthy father, who allegedly said that at age twenty-five John had worked only one week of his life. During seven years in college (from which he didn't graduate), his classmates said he spent much of his time simply watching television and eating junk food. After moving to the seamy Selma Avenue district of Los Angeles, he saw the movie *Taxi Driver,* which starred Jodie Foster as a prostitute. In the film, a loner incapable of communicating usually spends his spare time eating junk food and sitting in a dingy room. When this loner is scorned by Foster, he mails her a letter and sets out to kill a presidential candidate. John Hinkley, Jr. said he saw the film half a dozen times and became infatuated with Foster. After repeated attempts to see her failed, he decided to act out the plot of the movie and shoot the president.

Lee's mother was married three times. His father died a few months before his birth. His mother was a dominating woman who beat up her second husband and found it difficult to respond to anyone. Lee was rejected, yet tried to find self-esteem through the Marine Corps. Eventually he was court-martialed. He was skinny and balding. He married a woman who ridiculed him and made fun of his sexual impotency in front of a friend. Finally, he thought, his world of rejection would change. Taking a rifle to his job at a book-storage building, he fired two shells into the head of President John F. Kennedy.

Jim Golden is a young man in our Christian community. At one time he ran a pornographic magazine, controlled hundreds of prostitutes, used and sold drugs, killed a man in a street fight, and served three terms in prison. Ten years ago he was miraculously born again to Jesus Christ. Now he is one of eleven elders in a community of six hundred. Along with his wife and two gorgeous children, Jim is a trophy to the grace of God. His past is unusual but one fact stands out: Jim was the product of four broken homes.

The child is father to the man.

The home is the breeding ground for a person's future life.

The father is God's instrument to lead the way.

The Bible teaches that the father is the priest of the home. As a priest, he represents his family to God. In Hosea 4:6, another curse is listed when father-priests become renegades, reneging on their responsibility:

> My people are destroyed for lack of knowledge; because you have rejected knowledge, I reject you from being a priest to me. And since you have forgotten the law of your God, I also will forget your children.

Isn't our country today filled with what appears to be God-forgotten children? Not forgotten in the sense that God doesn't love them anymore, but forgotten in the sense that they seem so far from God's intention for their lives and so desperately in need of divine intervention.

In the very last paragraph of the Old Testament, this divine intervention is promised. And it also is pronounced amidst a curse:

> Behold, I am going to send you Elijah the prophet before the coming of the great and terrible day of the Lord. And he will restore the hearts of the fathers to their chil-

dren, and the hearts of the children to their fathers, lest I come and smite the land with a curse.

Malachi 4:5, 6 NAS

Here the Bible speaks prophetically about the end of the age. The urgent problem? Families divided; parents and children alienated from each other. What brings the curse? The divided-family situation left unattended and getting worse. The solution? It's twofold. First, the sending of an "Elijah ministry" to call for repentance and change. (Just as Jesus called John the Baptist "Elijah" in Matthew 17:11–13, He has promised to send others in the same spirit of Elijah at the end of the age.) The second part of the solution is fathers responding to the challenge by turning toward their children. The children also turn toward their fathers, *but only after the fathers make the first move.*

In Isaiah 59:16, we read that the Lord looked over a nation experiencing judgment and, "He saw that there was no man. . . ." In Ezekiel 22:30, a similar picture is painted of a nation in judgment: "I sought for a man . . . but I found none."

Today, I believe the Spirit of God is orchestrating a set of circumstances in our country to arrest our attention and blow an urgent trumpet in the midst of crisis times. In a day of cataclysmic change and great upheaval, in which we are witnessing the passing of the Christian era, the Lord is once again seeking "for a man."

I believe that if the church is going to launch a counteroffensive against the forces of darkness assaulting us and attempting to undermine our homes today, it will be because men rise to the challenge and spearhead the way. It will be because men proudly stand in their calling as husbands and fathers, provide loving leadership, and put their families at the top of their priorities.

Derek Prince, internationally known author and Bible teacher, has observed, "You may succeed in every other area of life, but if you fail as a father, then in God's eyes you are a failure at life."

Bill Gothard, nationally recognized seminar lecturer on the family and youth conflicts, has asserted, "We have weak churches because we have weak families. We have weak families because we have weak fathers. We have weak fathers because no one has taught them to be the spiritual leaders in their families."

Unless the father takes his place, accepts his responsibilities, and stands as God intends him to stand as the head of his home, the home will not be strong and healthy, and neither will our country. No society can last without stable family units.

When the question "Loving correction—who is responsible?" is raised, the answer should be obvious. God has charged men with the responsibility for providing loving leadership in the family. Like the Shepherd of the Twenty-third Psalm, the shepherd-father is to use the "staff" for guiding and the "rod" for correcting. Without question, the wife shares the responsibility, but the *primary* responsibility is on the father. In God's order there is no such thing as "I go to work and she raises the kids" or "I just can't take the responsibility anymore. You take it. I want out."

As the Apostle John wrote in 1 John 2:13, "I am writing to you, fathers. . . ."

And Paul wrote these words: "Fathers, do not provoke your children, lest they become discouraged" (Colossians 3:21).

"He [the father] must have proper authority in his own household, and be able to control and command the respect of his children" (1 Timothy 3:4 PHILLIPS).

"I will be his father, and he shall be my son. When he commits iniquity, I will chasten him with the rod of men, with the stripes of the sons of men" (2 Samuel 7:14).

". . . He commanded our fathers to teach to their children; that the next generation might know them, the children yet unborn, and arise and tell them to their children, so that they should set their hope in God, and not forget the works of God, but keep his commandments" (Psalms 78:5–7).

Abraham, the father of our faith, was chosen by God for one primary reason: God knew He could count on him as a husband and father: "I know him, that he will command his children and his household after him, and they shall keep the way of the Lord . . ." (Genesis 18:19 KJV).

Eli was rejected as a leader by God because he failed in his responsibility at home: "I tell him that I am about to punish his house for ever, for the iniquity which he knew, because his sons were blaspheming God, and *he did not restrain them*" (1 Samuel 3:13, my italics).

Likewise, David had family problems because he did not lovingly correct his son Adonijah with respect to his pride and rebellion. "Now Adonijah . . . exalted himself, saying, 'I will be king'; and he prepared for himself chariots and horsemen, and fifty men to run before him. *His father had never at any time displeased him by asking, 'Why have you done thus and so?'* " (1 Kings 1:5, 6, my italics).

These two examples of Eli and David are included in the Bible not to be cited as excuses for irresponsibility. ("Well, after all, even in the Bible there are some men whose families didn't turn out right.") They are there as sober warnings that we might learn from their mistakes.

We are privileged to see men responding to the Lord to "turn their hearts towards their children." Loving correction is a responsibility for both parents, but the father must take his rightful place of spiritual leadership.

When a man works late at his office, goes in on Saturdays, and reinvests his earnings back in the company, many admire his initiative, tenacity, and foresight. After all, this kind of sacrifice, inconvenience, mental and physical effort is absolutely essential in order to succeed. "Anything worth having demands hard work and great sacrifice." Why, then, are some surprised at the same kind of requirement to father a family?

Before we go on to the basic elements of loving correction, will you at this moment willingly accept your mantle (anointing) as a father and rise to the challenge?

1. *Recognize.* Be honest with yourself and the Lord in realizing your God-given charge and where you have failed. "No pains, no gains," says the familiar proverb.

2. *Repent.* Don't simply regret past mistakes and wallow in discouragement. Make a quality decision to change your direction now. Lou Brock, the major-league base-stealing record holder, has said, "Champions don't give up, they get up."

3. *Respond.* Embrace your God-given responsibility as husband, father, and spiritual leader. Take a *concrete first step* this very day to:

4. *Reorder priorities.* Sit down with your wife and reevaluate how your time is to be invested. There are no shortcuts. There's a price to pay. "Monday Night Football," involvement in sports, reading the evening paper—all must be evaluated in light of your family priority.

5. *Reach out.* Humble yourself to ask counsel from effective fathers. Have their families over and watch them in action. Ask them for fresh and creative ideas to use. "The intelligent man is always open to new ideas. In fact, he looks for them" (Proverbs 18:15 TLB).

Behold, I am going to send you Elijah the prophet before the coming of the great and terrible day of the Lord. And he will restore the hearts of the fathers to their children, and the hearts of the children to their fathers, lest I come and smite the land with a curse.

Malachi 4:5, 6 NAS

Review

1. Describe some aspects of judgment already being evidenced in our day.

2. What does it mean in Scripture by sons and daughters going "into captivity"?

3. Name the urgent problem at the end of the age cited in Malachi 4:5, 6.
4. What is the solution?
5. Who is ultimately responsible for loving correction in the home?
6. Name two biblical examples of fathers who failed with their sons.
7. Why are these two examples included in Scripture?

Response

If I am a father, have I accepted my position and responsibility in the home?

If I am a mother, how do I assist my husband in his role?

4

Loving: The Foundation

Loving stands by itself. Without it, there is no basis to go further. Love without correction is selfish indulgence. Correction without love is sterile indoctrination. One is foundational for the other. In order to have a healthy, well-balanced child, the key is to make sure the child feels loved. Dr. Ross Campbell, author of *How to Really Love Your Child*, expressed this thought: Make sure you always keep your child's emotional tank full!

Years ago, there was a study conducted to find out what happens to children living in an absence of love. Children who were confined to two different institutions were studied simultaneously. Both institutions were equivalent in all but one area: the amount of loving affection provided.

In one institution, labeled "Nursery," children were fondled, touched, picked up, spoken to, and so forth. After two years, the children proved absolutely normal in development, were healthy, and none died. In the other institution, called "Foundling Home," the infants were raised by a few nursing personnel so overworked that one nurse cared for up to twelve children. There was little demonstration of love. After only two years, the emotionally starved children were not able to speak, walk, or feed themselves. During a period of five years, there was a 37 percent mortality rate!

"Have you hugged your kid today?" is not just a cute cliché. It can be a matter of life and death.

If you have not committed yourself to keeping your child's emotional tank full, the implementation of the basic principles in this book will bring inevitable failure. You may have a prim and proper, well-behaved child in the early years, but you are courting disaster in the later years.

In order for a child to respond well to correction, we must give him what he needs. He can learn well only if he is happy, feels secure, and knows he is loved unconditionally. Even though we make a lot of mistakes as parents, if love prevails, it makes up for them. ". . . love covers a multitude of sins" (1 Peter 4:8).

On my VW dashboard is a bumper sticker: LOVE IS A VERB. In other words, love must be expressed in practical ways. It's not enough simply to have warm feelings toward children; parents must care enough to sacrifice whatever is needed for their best interest.

> . . . children ought not to lay up for their parents, but parents for their children. I will most gladly spend and be spent for your souls. If I love you the more, am I to be loved the less?
>
> 2 Corinthians 12:14, 15

Here Paul is not referring to financial investments. He's referring to parents laying down their lives and making personal investments of love in their children.

How can we translate our feelings of love into action and make sure our children feel loved? First of all, how are you presently viewing your children? Granted, children can get on one's nerves at times, and that's understandable. (Someone has defined *patience* as the art of idling your motor when you feel like stripping your gears!) Nevertheless, do you see them in a positive or in a negative light?

I still recall, when Justin was in his first month, how he seemed to have an uncanny, internal device which awakened him from his day of sleep precisely when we were retiring. He then proceeded to exercise his lungs for the next three or four hours straight, night after night after night. I remember standing at our front window—having tried every sleep-inducing technique I knew—thinking, *Lord, should I just throw him out?* Now, maybe you've never felt like that, but perhaps this will enable you to better understand those who have!

Seriously, what is your gut-level feeling toward your children? Do you see them as a bother? an infringement on your rights? an interruption in your life-style? a hindrance to the pursuit of your goals in life? an "accident"? another tax deduction? Even if you don't verbalize it to them, they're perceptive enough to pick up your spirit. This will color your relationship with them.

Howard G. Hendricks, a speaker in Family Life conferences and author of numerous books, asks: "Do you realize children are given not just for what you do for them, but for what they can do for you?"

Psalm 127 says that children should be viewed in three ways:

> Behold, children are a *gift* of the Lord; the fruit of the womb is a *reward*. Like *arrows* in the hand of a warrior, So are the children of one's youth. How blessed is the man whose quiver is full of them; They shall not be ashamed, When they speak with their enemies in the gate.
>
> Verses 3–5 NAS, my italics

1. *Children are a gift.* The Hebrew means "assignment." Do you see your children as a divine assignment and yourself as the responsible steward? You have the glorious opportunity of shaping the destiny of another human being. What a high calling in God!
2. *Children are a reward.* Imagine, the Grand Architect of the entire universe loves you so much as to make you a co-laborer with Him in the creation of life itself.
3. *Children are like arrows.* Why arrows? Because in order to be effective they have to be pointed in a certain direction. An arrow shot into the air at random is useless. Only as it flies toward its target does it serve a purpose. As parents, we have the marvelous opportunity of uncovering our children's unique gifts and calling, and then encouraging them into their divine placement in life.

A glass filled halfway with water can be viewed as half-empty or half-full. A pessimist views a difficulty in every opportunity; an optimist views an opportunity in every difficulty.

How are you viewing your children? Are they your delight? "The Lord reproves him whom he loves, as a father the son in whom he delights" (Proverbs 3:12).

If you sense rejection in your heart toward your child, confess your attitude to the Lord and then ask for the grace you need to begin learning to like your child. Titus 2:3, 4 says that older women are to "*train* the young women to love [*like* is the literal Greek] their . . . children" (my italics). It's a learning process. Begin to invest yourself and your time more in the child and you'll evidence a supernatural transformation. Jesus said, "Where your treasure is, there will your heart be also" (Matthew 6:21).

With a proper perspective on our children, we can examine some practical ways to make sure they feel loved and keep their emotional tank full.

In Matthew 18 is an account of a discussion Jesus had with the disciples on the subject of children. They asked Him:

> "Who is the greatest in the kingdom of heaven?" And calling to him a child, he put him in the midst of them, and said, "Truly, I say to you, unless you turn and become like children, you will never enter the kingdom of heaven. Whoever humbles himself like this child, he is the greatest in the kingdom of heaven."
>
> Verses 1–4

In other words, to be a part of the Kingdom of God, one must turn from his pride and exercise childlike faith in the Lord. This is "greatness" in the eyes of God. A secondary message is also conveyed: Don't take yourself too seriously! Stay childlike. Guard against sophistication which can suffocate your celebration of life.

In expressing love to our children, it's vital that we stay childlike and not take ourselves too seriously. (I believe one reason God gives us these "half-size gurus of play," as I have seen them referred to, is to remind us of this fact.) "A cheerful heart is a good medicine, but a downcast spirit dries up the bones" (Proverbs 17:22).

I need it as much as my son, Justin, when he shatters Daddy's reserve by "beeping" my belly button and I spin around the room like a top, again and again and again.

It's "good medicine" for us as a family when the "dude man" (one of Justin's nicknames) is being potty trained and every deposit is acclaimed by Mommy and Daddy hopping around the room, whistling, clapping, and cheering. As he proudly beams at us, he looks as if he just swallowed sunshine.

We need it as a family when Justin dives under Mommy and Daddy's bedcovers, wriggling through our legs like a snake, while our daughter, Melanie, bounces atop us like a frog.

A child feels loved when Mommy and Daddy can rediscover play, get down on his level, and act crazy once again. Dad and Mom may be firm, but they're also a lot of fun.

Prior to Justin's third birthday, he developed a strong fascination with drums. (Maybe it runs in the family. Before I became a Christian, I played drums for seven years

in a rock group called, ironically, the "Lost Souls.")
Watching the drummer in our Sunday meetings, Justin
decided he wanted to "have a meeting" in our living
room with him on the drums. Taking six assorted boxes,
some paper plates, two wooden spoons, and a whiffle-ball
bat, I managed to create a make-believe drum set.

Creation soon led to participation. Next thing I knew,
Justin had his daddy singing, clapping, dancing, and lifting his hands while he mercilessly slam-banged the boxes
from his percussion throne. This became our regular rou-
tine for months, especially when guests came to our
home. Talk about kissing self-consciousness good-bye! I
simply had to make a quality decision that my child's development meant more than my reputation in the eyes of
onlookers.

Jesus went on to say:

"Whoever receives one such child in my name receives
me; but whoever causes one of these little ones who believe in me to sin, it would be better for him to have a
great millstone fastened round his neck and to be
drowned in the depth of the sea."

Matthew 18:5, 6

When you wrestle with your child down on the floor
... when you tickle your child till her giggles fill the
house ... when you answer her seventy-fifth question of
the day ... when you leave "World News Tonight" to go
fix his truck—to whom are you ministering, according to
our Lord? Jesus Himself said, "to me" (Matthew 25:40).

And what does it mean to *receive* a child? The Greek

word means "to accept" or "to take to oneself." How, then, can you receive a child and thereby make sure he feels loved? Here are seven practical suggestions:

1. *Make sure you see your children as God sees them*—as a "gift," a "reward," and as "arrows"—not as an interruption, accident, or tax break (Psalms 127:3, 4 NAS).
2. *Cultivate a childlike attitude.* Don't take yourself too seriously. Rediscover play. Walk barefoot together across the wet grass. Ride a merry-go-round. Act out a story instead of merely reading it (Matthew 18:1–4).
3. *Give your children direct eye contact.* Jesus said that "the eye is the lamp of the body . . ." (Matthew 6:22). He calls us "the apple of his eye" (Deuteronomy 32:10). The Lord said, ". . . I will counsel you with my eye upon you" (Psalms 32:8). A child has a critical need for focused attention which enables him to feel respected, important, and loved. "Daddy (or Mommy) really cares about me . . . what I say . . . what I do."

Have you ever sat in a restaurant and watched a family relating? or should I say "not relating"? How often have you observed little children bobbing in their seats while sharing some exciting news while Dad, across the table, has his eyes glued to last night's box scores or is studying the assorted ways his french fries are arranged on the plate?

Children need to know we care. Sacrificing our present activity for a minute to practically demonstrate this will insure that our children feel loved. I believe "Love that is heard but not observed is absurd!"

4. *Physically express your love.* Regular hugging, kissing, sitting close together, tousling hair, tickling, rubbing backs (my son's favorite), putting an arm on the shoulder, a playful romp (not a slugfest)—all are absolutely essential to assure a child's emotional security and to nurture his self-esteem. They communicate this thought: "I like you and enjoy being with you." These are the building blocks of a strong, healthy love bond.

Howard Hendricks, a man of God I deeply respect, said that when his children were grown, he asked them what they remembered best from their childhood. He was somewhat surprised at their warmest memory, for they all said the same thing—when Dad would get down on the floor and wrestle with them!

Don't underestimate the potential of your children to recall events in their lives. I still remember the day a Christian brother, Bob Hoover, drove me to the Washington National Airport and I had my son along for the ride. Justin was two at the time. As I got out of the van, I slipped Bob a dollar, whispering that he could treat my son to an ice-cream cone at Baskin-Robbins before returning him home to his mom.

I totally forgot about the incident until seven months later, when I had a phone call from Bob early one morning.

"Daddy . . . Daddy . . . who ya talkin' to?" Justin chimed in while I was still on the phone.

"I'm talking to Bob Hoover."

"Who?"

"Bob Hoover."

"Oh, Bob who took me for ice cream after airport ride?"

Doing a double-take, I responded, "Yes," as I realized how sharp a child's memory can be.

Also, make it a point to lavish your children with daily encouragement. "Encourage one another day after day, as long as it is still called 'Today' ..." (Hebrews 3:13 NAS). Encourage them for tasks and meals completed; encourage them aloud before your friends (let them overhear you telling people on the phone how great they are); encourage them any and every chance you get!

5. *Train yourself to be a good listener.* Listening requires discipline, especially with children who can tell you the same Winnie the Pooh story a hundred times. It involves the eyes, ears, mind, and heart. It means kneeling at times so as to be on their level and to communicate eye to eye. It's important that as parents we respond to our child's feelings—"Rejoice with those who rejoice, weep with those who weep" (Romans 12:15)—and not *regularly* interrupt them or cut them off. Such statements as "Not now, I'm busy" or "Tell me later" say to a child: *I guess I'm not as important to Mommy and Daddy as other things are.*

Usually a child approaches a parent for one of four reasons: a) answers; b) affection; c) attention (to hurt or insecure feelings); d) association (companionship). We need to listen, not just to hear but also to understand and discern his or her point of need.

The moments just prior to saying good-night are usually an excellent time to hear a child's heart. For some strange reason, this seems to be the time when many children love to open up!

My wife and I found we were able to teach Justin most of his *A B C*s and how to count to ten (before he reached three years of age) by simply lying in bed with him for a few minutes before he fell asleep. During the same time span he also committed twelve Bible verses to memory. I don't cite this to boast but merely to underscore how valuable these "retiring" moments can be when used creatively.

Hear, O Israel: The Lord our God is one Lord: And thou shalt love the Lord thy God with all thine heart, and with all thy soul, and with all thy might. And these words, which I command thee this day, shall be in thine heart: And thou shalt teach them diligently unto thy children, and shalt talk of them when thou sittest in thine house, and when thou walkest by the way, *and when thou liest down,* and when thou risest up.

Deuteronomy 6:4–7 KJV, my italics

6. *Spend quality time together.* There simply is no substitute for regular, consistent time spent together doing ordinary things (eating, working, walking, praying, driving, swimming, shopping) or "making memories" by doing extraordinary things (visits to a zoo, pet shop, amusement park, or hospital; playing table games, attending a sandlot softball game; picnicking, camping, biking, hiking, building a model plane; sewing a doll's

outfit; sight-seeing, visiting museums, visiting your nearby fire station, and taking them for a tour of where Dad works).

A special "date" with each child on a regular basis—such as going to "Mickey D's" restaurant (McDonald's) or simply going for a walk together—is another idea.

While driving in the car, be alert to interesting sights and be flexible enough to stop. Coming upon a construction area, I often pull over for a minute so Justin and Melanie can check out the bulldozers and the dump trucks. (Isn't it amazing how bug-eyed little ones can get over the big earth-moving equipment?) Workers fixing city roads . . . men changing lamps on the street-lights . . . a homeowner chopping down a tree . . . two dogs chasing each other across the lawn, are all tailor-made for a child's curiosity. Children are inquisitive. Learn to capitalize on the novel, unique discoveries of everyday life.

Susanna Wesley had more than twenty children, yet she spent one hour with each child every week—listening, encouraging, and monitoring their spiritual progress. From these Wesley children emerged two men of God, John and Charles, who shook two continents for the Lord.

Obviously, all of this requires foresight and careful scheduling. Here again, the dad has the responsibility to take the initiative and pave the way.

Recently I took Justin out of the house for a few hours because his mom simply needed a little break. Driving past our corner fire station, I had an idea.

My boy is so fascinated by fire engines when they roar by the house that I thought, *Why not stop, go inside, and show him up close!*

Immediately I answered myself, "No. That's stupid. Firemen don't want the public coming inside their stations and snooping around. Besides, they're busy."

Maybe it's my bold nature or my sense of reckless abandonment, but I had a flash of inspiration and quickly jettisoned the negative thought. Spinning my car around, I turned into the drive thinking, *I can do this. After all, my taxes pay for this place.*

"Excuse me. Anybody here?" I said, upon walking inside with my son holding my hand.

A fellow with his feet propped up on his desk responded, "Yes. Can I help you?"

As I walked over to him I couldn't help but notice the TV room and the less-than-busy firemen.

"Sir, my boy really gets excited when he sees a fire engine go by. I was wondering if he might be able to look at one up close. Do you think it would be all right?"

Not only did I get a resounding "Sure!" with a smile, but next thing I knew, we had three personal escorts walking us through the station, lifting Justin in and out of fire engines, demonstrating equipment, and adjusting a fireman's helmet on his head. The farther along we went, the more I was convinced that we had added a lift to their humdrum day.

Justin talked about his fire-station visit for weeks. Each time he did, I had a fresh reminder of not only the significance of quality time together, but also of the numerous opportunities surrounding us if we'll simply keep our ears and eyes open.

Spending quality time with our children regularly must be a top priority. We can't expect the church to train them, for values are not so much taught as they are caught. Also, we can't cop out with a cliché like "It's not the quantity of time but the quality that counts," for the fact is that it's both. We can't rationalize by saying, "I'm too busy now, but I soon hope to be over the hump," for this is an illusion. Habit patterns are setting in, and deep down inside we know it.

The Bible prophesies that the last days will be characterized by people "running to and fro" (*see* Daniel 12:4) and Satan attempting to "wear out the saints" (Daniel 7:25). *With today's frenzied pace and fatiguing pressures, unless there burns in our hearts a deep biblical conviction concerning the priority of the family, we'll simply be seduced by the spirit of this age and one day awaken to regret it.*

Social scientists say we are now witnessing the demise of the family dinner hour in our American culture. And it's true. With today's rapid pace, working moms, television's impact, more and more people eating out, it's a rarity to have a family together and conversing over a meal for a significant period of time.

And the pace is picking up with frightening momentum. In dining out, a family used to park their car, settle inside, leisurely review a menu, and then relax for food and fellowship. Then the drive-in, fast-food chains emerged, and things got quicker. Today it's zip through a restaurant via the drive-in window. Tomorrow maybe we'll shout out our order and the food will be thrown in our window while we speed down the freeway!

Dr. James Dobson, a well-known author and lecturer on the family, recently cited a Cornell University study showing that middle-class fathers of preschool children spend, on the average, 37.7 *seconds* per day in real interaction with their youngsters. By contrast, the study indicates that children watch television approximately 54 *hours* per week.

Gordon MacDonald, in his penetrating book *The Effective Father*, cited an illustration of how one can underestimate the value of time invested in a child. He cited Boswell, the celebrated biographer of Samuel Johnson, who often reminisced about an experience in his childhood when his dad took him fishing. Boswell recalled many memories and lessons learned from that special time spent with his dad. Because one person had heard of this event so often, he decided to check the journal of Boswell's father to see just how his dad himself recorded the day. Upon discovering the entry, the individual found a simple sentence: "Gone fishing today with my son; a day wasted."

How easy it is to overlook what, to a child, is so important.

We must come to grips with the significance of regular quality time with our children. Just as a businessman starts a company and sees his future corporation through the "eye of faith," so, too, must we make investments in our children with a view toward the future. Remember: IT IS BETTER TO BUILD CHILDREN THAN TO REPAIR MEN.

At home I have a record with prophetic lyrics that, when heard one day, stopped me in my tracks. It's been widely quoted by many today who see our societal trends and share a burden for families.

Cat's in the Cradle
Harry and Sandy Chapin

My child arrived just the other day;
he came to the world in the usual way.
But there were planes to catch and bills to pay;
he learned to walk while I was away.
And he was talkin' 'fore I knew it, and as he grew
he'd say, "I'm gonna be like you, Dad,
you know I'm gonna be like you."

And the cat's in the cradle and the silver spoon.
Little boy blue and the man in the moon.
"When you comin' home, Dad?"
"I don't know when, but we'll get together then.
You know we'll have a good time then."

My son turned ten just the other day;
he said, "Thanks for the ball, Dad. Come on, let's play.
   Can you teach me to throw?"
I said, "Not today. I got a lot to do."
He said, "That's okay."
And he walked away, but his smile never dimmed,
it said, "I'm gonna be like him, yeah,
you know I'm gonna be like him."

And the cat's in the cradle and the silver spoon.
Little boy blue and the man in the moon.

"When you comin' home, Dad?"
"I don't know when, but we'll get together then.
You know we'll have a good time then."

Well, he came from college just the other day;
so much like a man, I just had to say,
"Son, I'm proud of you; can you sit for a while?"
He shook his head and he said with a smile,
"What I'd really like, Dad, is to borrow the car keys. See
    you later. Can I have them, please?"

And the cat's in the cradle and the silver spoon.
Little boy blue and the man in the moon.
"When you comin' home, Dad?"
"I don't know when, but we'll get together then.
You know we'll have a good time then."

I've long since retired. My son's moved away.
I called him up just the other day.
I said, "I'd like to see you, if you don't mind."
He said, "I'd love to, Dad, if I can find the time.
You see my new job's a hassle and the kids have the flu,
but it's sure nice talkin' to you, Dad.
It's been sure nice talkin' to you."

And as I hung up the phone, it occurred to me,
he'd grown up just like me.
My boy was just like me.

And the cat's in the cradle and the silver spoon.
Little boy blue and the man in the moon.
"When you comin' home, son?"
"I don't know when, but we'll get together then.
You know we'll have a good time then."

How about you?

During your children's formative years, when they are so pliable and vulnerable, will you—dads and moms—turn your hearts toward your children?

The final way to receive a child and make sure he feels loved is:

7. *Exercise loving correction in faith.* Since I've already covered the importance of faith and the significance of loving, let us now turn the spotlight on correction in the following section.

Review

1. What is the place of love in correcting our children, and why?
2. Explain the significance of the slogan "Have you hugged your kid today?"
3. Psalm 127 speaks of three ways to view our children. Name and explain them.
4. What does Jesus mean by "turn and become like children" in Matthew 18?
5. Name ways to receive a child and thereby make sure he feels loved.
6. What is meant by "spending quality time together?"
7. Respond to "It's not the quantity of time but the quality that counts."

Response

Which of the elements of receiving a child do I need to concentrate on with my children?

5

Correction: The Basic Elements

Scores of parents recognize the importance of loving correction but have no idea how it can be implemented in their homes. The following acrostic is provided so you'll have a foothold for easy remembrance. Learn it. Let it be a ready resource for your situation as well as something to share with inquiring friends. When people observe your well-behaved children, they're going to ask questions. You need to be prepared with articulate responses to their honest questions. One tip: Work on a few of these principles at a time and don't expect immediate results. Move in faith and patience, ". . . for in due season we shall reap, if we do not lose heart" (Galatians 6:9).

Clarity
Obedience
Right Attitudes
Restoration
Explanation
Consistency
Thoroughness
Immediately
Out-of-Sight
Neutral Object

Years ago, I sensed a serious deficiency in my life. The area was self-discipline. My exercising was inconsistent. I was habitually tardy, and procrastination (putting off till tomorrow what's already been put off till today) was dominating entire areas of my life.

While walking through an airport, I passed a bookrack containing a volume which caught my eye: *The Disciplined Life* by Richard S. Taylor. I continued twenty paces farther until I did an about-face, sensing as I did the "finger of God" propelling me back to the bookrack.

Later, on the plane, I fanned the pages of my new book until I come back to the table of contents. Chapter headings like "Discipline the Key to Power" and "Discipline the Mark of Maturity" intrigued me. Scanning downward, my eyes finally became riveted on the juicy title, "How to Become a Disciplined Person."

Quickly turning to the latter part of the book, I dug in:

Begin by reading the entire book through, including the Introduction, if you have not already done so. Some of you will spot the title of this chapter while scanning the Contents and, recognizing that becoming a disciplined person is the goal, will suppose that to read only this chapter will be sufficient. Such an attempt may be symptomatic of your need of discipline.

Gulp.

If you have done a similar thing in turning to this section to begin your reading, please go back to the beginning.

Earlier in the book I made this statement:

> Correction cannot be divorced from the context of a
> strong, healthy love bond between parents and child. If
> you have not committed yourself to keeping your child's
> emotional tank full, the implementation of the basic
> principles in this book will bring inevitable failure. You
> may have a prim and proper, well-behaved child in the
> early years, but you are courting disaster in the later
> years.

Now if you *have* been reading from the start, let's continue. Here are two important points before we survey the
basic elements of correction.

First, loving correction will involve an investment of
time. Larry Christenson, in his book *The Christian Family*, cites a Christian parent as declaring that "spanking is an event." In other words, a parent does not
simply haul off and "nail" a child because of reaching
the breaking point. Loving correction has nothing to
do with this quick and easy, yet cruel and unbiblical
approach.

Second, loving correction should be started early. It
may not be full-blown initially (using a simple finger flick
when anger or rebellion is discerned), but wise parents
will not procrastinate. The reason parents experience the
so-called Terrible Twos is that attitudes which were never
dealt with before now surface.

"Discipline your son in his early years while there is
hope. If you don't you will ruin his life" (Proverbs 19:18
TLB). "When I was a son with my father, tender, the only

one in the sight of my mother, he taught me . . ." (Proverbs 4:3, 4).

Setting an arbitrary age for beginning isn't my intention. I would suggest you ask the Lord to alert you when the time has come.

Couples in our Christian fellowship, and numerous others I have taught in, usually begin somewhere between nine and eighteen months. It may sound early, but over the years we've seen the positive results with scores of children. (Remember we are talking of dealing with *discerned rebellion,* not crying due to gas, sickness, hunger, discomfort, and so forth.)

Before his first birthday, Justin was corrected on two occasions for trying to manipulate Doris and me by screaming. Knowing his needs were completely met, we observed him scream when Daddy exited and then laugh upon his return. Over and over he did this, disregarding our firm *nos.* Finally, we accompanied the *no* with a firm finger flick on the thigh. After a few times, we saw the results.

If you're a late starter, don't be discouraged. You've walked in the light that you've had. Now begin where you are, even if it means asking forgiveness of your children and explaining to them your new commitment to Christ and His Word. Move in wisdom and trust in His promise: "I will restore to you the years that the locust hath eaten . . ." (Joel 2:25 KJV). Don't dare succumb to the lie "It's too late; it'll never work now." That thought is not from God and must be rejected immediately. ". . . with

God all things are possible" (Matthew 19:26).

Here, then, are the basic elements of loving correction:

Clarity

Loving correction always begins by clearly defining reasonable boundaries *before* they are enforced. Just as God sets boundaries concerning how we're to live (boundaries which have definite consequences if violated), so, too, must we do the same. This brings security.

Establishing limits—especially with small children—entails more than verbal instruction stated just once. ". . . To write the same things to you is not irksome to me, and is safe for you" (Philippians 3:1). It means regular reminders (little ones forget easily), asking for a response when the child's old enough to give one ("Is that clear?"), and modeling desired behavior.

Doris and I have found it effective to be somewhat dramatic in modeling desired behavior for little ones. Children get bug-eyes when you demonstrate with exaggerated gestures and sounds: "Socket is noooo, nooo, nooo [moving hand toward wall]. And if you disobey . . . ooowww . . . ooowww . . . ooowww [acting out the applied correction]."

We also found it helpful when Justin and Melanie Ann were very young to use certain brief phrases *repeatedly* rather than different ones for the same activity. For example, when it was time for Justin or Melanie to stop wriggling and talking and go to sleep, we'd repeatedly say, "Head down!" This promotes greater clarity than using different phrases such as, "Okay, it's time to go to sleep" one time and, "Stop talking and fall asleep" the next.

Know that it's within a child to challenge boundaries. This is his way of testing your authority. It's also his way of drawing security from your love. Someone has compared it to a night watchman's testing doors to see if they're locked. He's attempting to open the doors, but he wants them to be locked. Likewise, a child, in testing his boundaries, is saying by his actions, "Is it secure? Am I 'locked in' to your love?"

Two criteria I'd suggest for setting boundaries would be: a) *boundaries to protect others*—hitting another child, swiping a sister's cookie, throwing a ball in the house, and so forth; and b) *boundaries to protect self*—touching appliances, medicine, and sockets; observing bedtime hours, eating what is served, and so on.

Loving correction is always based on reasonable boundaries that are clearly defined in advance.

Obedience and Right Attitudes

These two elements of loving correction need to be examined together. They are the two main areas we, as parents, are to work on with our children. *When the rod of correction is applied, it's because a child has displayed either willful disobedience or wrong attitudes.*

Scripture teaches, "Children, obey your parents in the Lord, for this is right" (Ephesians 6:1). Roy Lessin, author of *How to Be the Parents of Happy and Obedient Children,* says that our children should obey "willingly, completely and immediately." These are three excellent criteria to follow. If violated, our responsibility is loving correction.

Willingly. Scripture teaches we are to "do all things without grumbling or questioning" (Philippians 2:14), and to "serve the Lord with gladness! . . ." (Psalms 100:2). How we parents must be on our toes about this one! ("Daddy, how come you look so grumpy tonight? I thought you said. . . .")

Completely. Scripture directs, "Children, obey your *parents in everything,* for this pleases the Lord" (Colossians 3:20, my italics).

This means that *all* of the room is cleaned—not half—and all the toys are put back—not all of them except three.

Immediately. The Bible says that when Jesus called the disciples, "Immediately they left their nets and followed him" (Matthew 4:20). This means that when we tell our children something, they are trained to obey us the first time we speak; they come the first time they are called. No threatening, yelling, or debating. *Delayed obedience is disobedience.* (Clarity is essential here. Was the command clear and audible?) Evidently, this is how the boy Samuel was trained, for he responded at the first call every time (1 Samuel 3:1–21). He could easily have excused himself from getting out of bed so late at night, especially after the first couple of false alarms.

Doris and I were adjusted on this point by friends in another Christian fellowship. (We have verbalized to numerous Christian couples that they should take the liberty of "speaking the truth" [Ephesians 4:15] to us about any shortcomings or blind spots which they perceive in us.) Paul and Anna shared with us that we're the ones who ultimately choose the number of times it takes for our child to respond. If we call two times and then try a third with a firm "I said come here!" we're simply training the child to come on the third command. ("Oh, oh, I'd better go. Now I think Daddy means it.") My friend Paul stated, "Never repeat your command. Be gracious to say, 'What did Daddy say?' but don't train your child to delay obedience. One day you could regret it." Paul then went on to relate a true story of a little boy whose life was saved because he immediately stopped when his daddy commanded, "Timmy! Stop!" At the time, he was only a few yards from oncoming traffic! ". . . keep my commandments, and live" (Proverbs 4:4).

I remember how my mother used to call me for supper when I was a little boy. I'd be playing basketball in a yard three houses away when I'd hear my mom call, "Larry, it's time for dinner."

"Be there in a minute," I'd respond, and simply continue to play.

Five or ten minutes later, I'd be in the middle of a jump shot when again I'd hear a firmer, "Larry! I said it's time for dinner!"

"Okay, I'm almost there."

"Hurry up, guys," I'd usually say, "I gotta get going pretty soon."

Five minutes later, my mother (or maybe this time my father) would shriek at lung's capacity, "Larry! You'd better get in this house *this* minute!"

"That's it guys. I have to split. Now they mean business."

Off I'd go, running home like a bobcat.

If this happened once, it happened a hundred times.

The problem was delayed obedience. Remember: Delayed obedience is disobedience.

It is essential that we view these three criteria as our *goals* and not demand instant compliance during the early period of training. It takes a while for a child to learn these responses. We have found it helpful to get the child's attention and "freeze the picture" to allow the child to choose obedience rather than his natural impulse. Example: If a young child is playing with something and you want him to give it to you, rather than a quick "Give it to me" and an instant spanking if he does not, afford him maximum opportunity to make the right choice. Get his attention first. Then say, "Billy, Mommy wants you to give her the empty glass." The child clearly knows what you want and he is faced with a decision. If you sense he is hesitating, feel free to add, "Billy, you must obey. If you don't, then you will get the rod." (Obviously, we are speaking here of smaller children in the early stages of training. With older children, or when a child is trained properly, immediate obedience should mean exactly that—*immediate.*)

It is also important to discern the difference between willful disobedience and childishness. Scripture does say, "When I was a child ... I reasoned like a child ..." (1 Corinthians 13:11). Children are children, not full-fledged adults. They will accidently spill milk, act silly, forget to bring in something out of the rain, and so forth. Here's where our understanding and tolerance comes in.

Not only are we to concentrate on obedience but on right attitudes as well. "Serve the Lord with gladness! ..." declares the Bible (Psalms 100:2). It also observes that "... man looks on the outward appearance, but the Lord looks on the heart" (1 Samuel 16:7). Sulking, whining, fussing, arching one's back defiantly, pouting, complaining, holding the breath until the child turns blue—these are all evidence of a wrong attitude, and warrant the rod of correction after clear instruction. Even withdrawal and refusal to greet people when told to do so ("Say 'hi' to Uncle Steve, Justin." "No.") can be eliminated to produce healthy, happy children. (NOTE: Please don't dismiss this kind of behavior as merely "a stage" he's going through.)

Years ago, I heard a story about a little boy and his dad in a Christian meeting. "Sit down," said the father to his son, who was standing upright in his seat. As the boy slumped to his seat, obviously displeased, he glared at his dad and retorted, "I may be sitting down on the outside, but on the inside I'm still standing up!"

Outward obedience is not enough. God looks at the heart, and so must we.

Whenever Justin walks around with a sour expression

on his face, Doris and I immediately say to him, "Justin, take off the grumpy face and put on a happy face." We've trained him to pretend he's casting off the unhappy face mask and then replacing it with one having a smile.

When Justin was sixteen months old, he would awaken from his naps cranky and whiny. Then one day we realized we could help him overcome his wrong attitude. Prior to his nap, Daddy got down on his knees and imitated the way Justin was presently awakening. Repeating "bad attitude" throughout my Academy Award-winning performance, I shook my head and said, "Nooo."

When Justin later awoke and began his "rumblings," we stationed ourselves outside his door and I said, "Mommy, isn't it nice that Justin will be a happy baby when we go see him? No more bad attitude. Nooo! Justin serves the Lord with gladness."

If only it were this easy every time! As we opened the door, there he was—the "dude man"—standing wide-eyed and wearing his silly little grin.

Little children know what's going on. Don't let them fool you!

When Justin was fourteen months old, he developed a bad attitude toward us as we lovingly corrected him. We dismissed it for a while, but then realized it was not of God. The problem? As we'd talk to him about his offense, he'd stubbornly refuse to look at us.

About this time, I left for ministry in South Africa, and so my wife took on the project of breaking Justin of this habit. After numerous sessions where Doris applied loving correction (with appropriate communication and affection each time), she finally achieved success. Upon my return, she demonstrated the fruits of her labors and we praised God together.

Is Justin a strong-willed child? Is the ocean wet?

Raising children for God is certainly one of the most challenging yet most rewarding tasks there is. Nothing else can so cause a person to cry out to God for assistance on a moment-by-moment basis. That's the way He intends it to be.

Obedience and right attitudes. These are the two major focal points of our "assignment" as parents.

Before moving on to the next point, let me take a moment to address an area that often perplexes parents. It's the subject of "thumb sucking." Is a child disobeying or displaying a bad attitude if you feel he should stop, yet he or she persists? Or better yet, should we even try to get children to stop sucking on thumbs?

From all the studies I've seen on the subject, most dentists say you should simply ignore thumb sucking until your child is around four and a half or five years old. Trying to break the habit prematurely can cause psychological problems. Most children stop sucking their thumbs by their first year in school, so there's no need to worry about bite problems, protruding teeth, or speech problems.

After five years of age, if the habit continues, here's what I'd suggest:

First, pray to your heavenly Father, in the name of

Jesus, that He will sovereignly begin to remove your child's desire for thumb sucking. Pray in faith. Remember these promises:

> And Jesus answering saith unto them, Have faith in God. For verily I say unto you, That whosoever shall say unto this mountain, Be thou removed, and be thou cast into the sea; and shall not doubt in his heart, but shall believe that those things which he saith shall come to pass; he shall have whatsoever he saith. Therefore I say unto you, What things soever ye desire, when ye pray, believe that ye receive them, and ye shall have them. And when ye stand praying, forgive, if ye have ought against any: that your Father also which is in heaven may forgive you your trespasses. But if ye do not forgive, neither will your Father which is in heaven forgive your trespasses.
>
> Mark 11:22–26 KJV

> If ye abide in me, and my words abide in you, ye shall ask what ye will, and it shall be done unto you.
>
> John 15:7 KJV

> Ask, and it shall be given you; seek, and ye shall find; knock, and it shall be opened unto you: For every one that asketh receiveth; and he that seeketh findeth; and to him that knocketh it shall be opened. Or what man is there of you, whom if his son ask bread, will he give him a stone? Or if he ask a fish, will he give him a serpent? If ye then, being evil, know how to give good gifts unto your children, how much more shall your Father which is in heaven give good things to them that ask him?
>
> Matthew 7:7–11 KJV

Then, use this one-month plan suggested by Dr. Richard Parmley of Cardinal Glennon Hospital for Children in Saint Louis, Missouri:

1. Using heavy poster paper and bright colors, make a twenty-eight-day calendar-style chart with seven spaces across and four down. Date the first box for the morning after the test begins. Buy stick-on stars, including several gold ones.
2. Thread ribbons into the tops of a pair of heavy wool socks, size eight or larger.
3. Do not allow the child to eat or drink two hours before bedtime, and make sure he or she goes to the bathroom right before being tucked into bed so he will sleep undisturbed.
4. Slip the socks, while he or she is asleep, on the child's hands like mittens, and tie them behind and above the elbows.
5. If both socks are in place in the morning, put a star in the first box. For one sock, use a half star.
6. If a child gets seven full stars in the week, use a gold one the last day, and continue the method for three more weeks.
7. Four gold stars at the end of the month indicate no psychological dependence, and the habit probably will have been broken. But a psychologically dependent child will have pulled the socks off without suffering emotional damage.

If you use this plan, remember you must proceed in faith and your faith is not in a method or a man but in your Maker. "Without faith it is impossible to please him.

For whoever would draw near to God must believe that he is [faithful, loyal, consistent, covenant-keeping] and that *he rewards those who seek him diligently"* (*see* Hebrews 11:6).

Restoration

This element should be self-explanatory. In correcting our child, our objective is never to leave him or her feeling guilty, rejected, or unwanted. Our intention is to deal immediately with the problem behavior and then restore fellowship. This is how God deals with us and we are to follow suit.

> If we confess our sins, he is faithful and just, and will forgive our sins and cleanse us from all unrighteousness.
> 1 John 1:9

> Come, let us return to the Lord; for he has torn, that he may heal us; he has stricken, and he will bind us up.
> Hosea 6:1

> You should rather turn to forgive and comfort him, or he may be overwhelmed by excessive sorrow. So I beg you to reaffirm your love for him.
> 2 Corinthians 2:7, 8

Even though we display grief in our facial expression to reflect the seriousness of the wrong, *we are not to continue on after administering the rod and securing repentence.* A child needs to be released from guilt by our words and actions. Embrace him and reassure him of your love and forgiveness. Rock him gently (children are very "clingy" after correction). Don't send the child to his room. Let him continue his activities, with an education under his belt. Never say, "Oh, you poor thing. Mommy (or Daddy) didn't mean it." This simply cancels out the lesson.

"Justin, now look at Daddy. You know how much I love you, but when you don't obey, Jesus teaches that you must receive the rod. Now are you sorry you disobeyed [or had a bad attitude]?" Upon acknowledgment (nodding or verbal), I continue, "Are you going to obey and be a good boy? Good. Then Jesus forgives you and Daddy forgives you, and everything is all better. I love you. . . ."

After hugs and a kiss, Justin is on his merry way—*secure* in my love and *liberated* from all feelings of guilt and rejection. The episode is *over.*

When a child is too young to respond with a nod or verbal "yes," still go through some variation of the above to train both the little one and yourself as well.

When a child is older and begins talking in phrases, expand on the above as you desire. Let him acknowledge with his own lips the wrong; pray together. Do whatever works best for you and your unique child.

Isn't this far better than "worldly" ways of dealing with children's misbehavior? There a child is often the object of verbal abuse or uncontrolled smacks, and then left to feel condemned. The overwhelming sense of injustice a child feels develops into resentment and bitterness. Parents and child both lose.

Explanation

Never leave a child confused as to why the rod is being applied. This only brings frustration and negates the lesson you want learned. A moment of communication is essential (even if you feel the little one is too young to understand). Besides, taking time for an explanation also gives you the chance to calm down if you need it!

In a non-accusing manner ask the child, "What did you do?" (If the child is too young, you tell him.) The purpose is to clarify the offense in the child's mind. Don't ask, "Did you do it?" (if you *know* he did). This only encourages him to try to deny the felt accusation. Simply ask him, *"What did you do?"*

Besides quickly identifying the wrong, the explanation aids the child in understanding that you're not against him. You're merely correcting a wrong action.

One final point. As parents, we shouldn't argue with our children concerning the limits set on their behavior. ("Because *I* said so." "But why?" "Because *I'm* the boss here!" "But why? ...") Arguing undermines our authority. It also suggests weakness, indecision, and uncertainty.

Consistency

"Mommy, can I have a few more oatmeal cookies?"
"No, honey, not now. You've had enough today."
"Oh, please . . . can't I have some?"

"No, Mommy already said no."

"Just a few?"

"I said no."

"Come on, I'll only have one or two."

"No!"

"Mommy." (Manipulative tears are now turned on.)

"Well, okay. But only take two."

"Daddy . . . how come you won't let me play with it? Mommy does."

Tuesday: "Now Billy, remember what I tell you. You are not to climb on top of these swings."

Wednesday: "So glad you called, Marge. No, I have time. I'm done fixing dinner and Billy's outside [looking out the window] climbing on the swings." *Should I stop and go out there? I just sat down . . . oh, I can let it go.*

Inconsistency. That's what the examples above demonstrate. Nothing can so frustrate a child and undercut effective child rearing as this bad habit. ". . . he who loves him [his son] is *diligent* to discipline him" (Proverbs 13:24, my italics).

The word *diligent* here speaks of a realization that loving correction requires day-by-day effort, and it reflects a persevering commitment to do the job. There are no shortcuts. Starting is easy; sticking is hard!

God Himself is consistent, and that is what gives us security as His children.

We, too, must make a quality commitment to be consistent if we want our children to be secure. (Both parents must agree on this commitment as well as on the rules of the house. If ever a disagreement arises, both parents should withdraw to another room and come to one mind!)

The reason a "quality commitment to be consistent" is imperative is so that we have an *anchor* when we're tempted to "let it go—just this once." Times will come when the easier route is to forego correction because we are physically or emotionally tired. (*Oh, I just sat down to relax.*) Or we are not at home but at the home of a relative, in a restaurant, or in a supermarket. (*What will they think?*) Or the child doesn't seem to feel well. (This definitely requires greater compassion, but consistency still must hold where possible.)

Settle it now, once and for all, that we as parents will not allow laziness, inconvenience, or the "fear of man" to hinder us in being totally consistent in the loving correction of our children.

If we violate this commitment (and such times will come!), we understand that we need to confess it as sin (and ask the child's forgiveness, too!). Consistent correction is God's command: "Whoever knows what is right to do and fails to do it, for him it is sin" (James 4:17). Loving correction of our children is not simply a good idea. It is God's holy plan for us to follow faithfully:

When we're just stepping out of the shower and it would be easier to forget it.

When we're watching "the game," and it's fourth quarter with "third and goal to go."

When we're with Grandma and Grandpa, and one says, "Oh, we wouldn't think of hitting poor baby for that."

Before you ever leave your child with grandparents—or anyone—make sure you sit down and go over the ground rules. If there's disagreement, respectfully submit that you have chosen to discipline differently from them and that if they want to take care of him, they'll have to abide by your rules. Even though Scripture says that "grandchildren are the crown of the aged ..." (Proverbs 17:6), it also records, "For this reason a man shall *leave* his father and mother ..." (Matthew 19:5, my italics). If you neglect this counsel, you'll not only reap at home the fruit of your compromise but you'll also provoke your children into discouragement. As Colossians 3:21 says, "Fathers, do not provoke your children, lest they become discouraged."

When you are leaving your children with someone else, keep in mind your responsibility to educate both the children and the sitter. This is essential to maintain consistency in the home. Some practical suggestions:

1. *Transfer authority to those assuming responsibility for your children in front of the children.* "Justin and Melanie, I want you to obey Elaine while Mommy and Daddy are away. We are going to a meeting and will be home in a few hours. Elaine will give us a full report when we come home."

2. *Make sure your children have had sufficient time to interact with the sitter.* Also, make sure the sitter has had sufficient time observing you as a couple raising your children. (Obviously a Christian man or woman or Christian couple is essential here so that biblical values and convictions are upheld.)

3. *Leave the phone number where you can be contacted.*

4. *Decide whether you want to delegate authority to the sitter to administer correction in your absence.* Again, make sure the sitter is thoroughly familiar with your approach and has been supervised by you in the carrying out of disciplinary measures. Should you decide that no one but you will correct your children, insure that your child knows offenses will be reviewed and dealt with when Daddy comes home.

5. *Assume responsibility for the children's creative activity in your absence.* Inform the sitter of your program of creative activity for the evening: coloring, drawing, Bible stories, athletics, and so on.

6. *Visualize possible difficulties and give specific suggestions for handling.* "Elaine, Justin already had ice cream at dinner, so no more while we're away. Do you understand that, too, little man?"

7. *Pray with your children and the sitter before departing.* Putting your blessing on your little ones in leaving seals the evening in God's loving care. Notice how many times in the New Testament Jesus placed His hands upon children and imparted a blessing.

One additional sidelight is worth mentioning at this time. With a house full of company, *always assign one person the responsibility* to watch your child if you are busy with food preparation or welcoming guests. All too often people politely volunteer to watch a child but, after becoming involved in conversation, tend to forget. Even if you have to leave your child alone for only a few minutes, don't leave things in the general, "Keep an eye on her, okay?" By assigning the responsibility to just one person, you can avert an unnecessary accident or tragedy. (Three years ago I met a father in Florida who tearfully related to me how his ten-month-old son was killed when he slipped away from a family celebration and crawled down the driveway, right into the path of an oncoming truck.)

Consistency is an element of loving correction that must permeate every facet of our parenting responsibilities.

When Justin was about eighteen months old, he accompanied me to a Christian conference. While walking through a parking lot at the motel, Justin decided he no longer would hold my hand while we walked (something Doris and I had trained him to do, and which he had been doing very well until this point).

"Justin," Daddy said, "give me your hand." Stubbornly recoiling, Justin refused. He was defiantly challenging my authority.

Giving him grace, I said, "What did Daddy say?"

What followed in the parking lot was a series of repeated spankings (with explanation and abundant display of affection between each one), until he finally realized that Daddy always wins and *wins decisively!*

As we walked on, hand in hand, a lady who had been watching the entire scene stopped me by asking, "Ah . . . does that little child need his mommy [projecting guilt all over me]? I couldn't help but hear him!"

Sensing that this lady viewed me as a candidate for charges of child abuse, I politely thanked her for her concern and explained to her what had just transpired. I also used the occasion to share with her my commitment to Jesus Christ and biblical principles for child rearing. Even though she didn't agree, I felt she understood by the time I was done.

It's times like this, when the public is watching, that one is tempted to compromise. (I know one mother who received a sharp "That's disgusting!" as she corrected her son outside a food store.) Yet, if we see correction as a matter of obedience to God and understand how crucial consistency is, we'll uphold our commitment in the face of all opposition.

Close friends of ours eventually saw one set of their parents won to Christ, partly through an "explanation session" on child correction. Grandma and Grandpa, noticing their grandchild's superb behavior, asked questions which led our friends to share their convictions about Jesus Christ and the Word of God. A needed reconciliation took place between the woman and her parents, which later paved the way for their commitment to Jesus Christ.

One last point. Some parents are ensnared by thinking children should be spanked a few times for an offense, but then let go if there is no change. This simply encourages children to "stick it out" because eventually they'll emerge the victors.

Be consistent!

Print this on a three-by-five-inch card and post it in various parts of your house. The dividends are worth the investment.

Thoroughness

In loving correction, our intention is always to *curb assertive self-will but not crush the spirit.* We are trying to shape the child's will. We don't want a broken spirit.

> A man's spirit will endure sickness; but a broken spirit who can bear?
>
> Proverbs 18:14

> A cheerful heart is a good medicine, but a downcast spirit dries up the bones.
>
> Proverbs 17:22

Have you ever seen a little child who has been unjustly reprimanded by someone? or a child who's been verbally humiliated? "You brat! You'll never amount to anything. You're a monster! I wish I'd never had you!"

"There is one whose rash words are like sword thrusts . . ." (Proverbs 12:18).

To shape the will without breaking the spirit, there must be thoroughness in our correction. The rod is used to "sting" instead of giving the traditional "love pats" which everyone knows to be ineffective. "Chasten thy son while there is hope, and let not thy soul spare for his crying" (Proverbs 19:18 KJV).

Our use of the rod must be *effective correction.* It must bring the child to a point of repentance and not merely "feeling sorry for getting caught." We need to train ourselves to hear the *repentant* cry, not just a contrived cry or a cry of protest. We need to discern that our child's cry is conveying, "I'm sorry. I won't do it again."

"How long should I spank?"

This varies with every child, depending on his or her sensitivity. Some children have a little more "padding," and are strong willed, so they need a longer spanking. Others are docile and easily start the process of repentance upon a stern look from Daddy or Mommy. (Don't use this as an excuse, though, for not completing the job!)

Although it's not possible to establish a "kiloswats" measurement for spanking, two biblical criteria are helpful. *Loving correction should be painful:* "For the moment all discipline seems painful rather than pleasant ..." (Hebrews 12:11). There can be no effective correction if our children giggle, laugh, or play when they are receiving the rod. *Loving correction should also yield the peaceful fruit of righteousness* "to those who have been trained by it" (Hebrews 12:11). If we have properly administered loving correction, we will see the eventual evidence of righteous behavior and not merely tears: "Even a child makes himself known by his acts, whether what he does is pure and right" (Proverbs 20:11).

"What if my child repeatedly disobeys during the course of a day and some redness develops on his bottom?"

Keep in mind that "posterior protoplasmic stimulation" can cause some redness on the skin. This is nothing to get upset about! These marks are only temporary. It's better for a child to have a few temporary marks outside than to retain improper attitudes inside that can leave permanent scars later in life. Remember: *If you permit a child to nurture a habit which he will one day be forced (with greater difficulty) to break, you are the cruelest of parents.*

Loving correction is to be thorough. By so doing, we curb the self-will without crushing the spirit.

Immediately

> Because sentence against an evil deed is not executed speedily, the heart of the sons of men is fully set to do evil.
>
> Ecclesiastes 8:11

Loving correction needs to be given immediately. As soon as possible. Promptly. Not "when Daddy comes home" or "when we get home" or "after we're done eating." (A *rare* exception may indeed arise.)

The reasons are obvious.

First, if we delay in correcting the wrong action or attitude, our tolerance level drops. Because of neglect, we find ourselves finally reacting out of frustration and anger rather than responding out of obedience and calm self-control. (This is something Doris and I both have slipped into at times and have had to repent immediately.)

Second, children have short memory spans and easily forget the reason for the correction.

Third, the temptation will later be there to simply drop the whole thing, especially if the child has "remarkably" improved his behavior.

Finally, a child shouldn't have to carry around in him the weight of an expected but delayed spanking. He deserves a rapid release so that he can quickly repent and be restored. When out in public, promptly utilize bathroom stalls, phone booths, out-of-the-way corridors, or even return to your automobile, if possible.

When I was little, my parents (whom I love dearly and who will be the first to acknowledge their earlier lack of training regarding biblical principles of correction), used to tell my sister and me that we were going to get it when we got home from Sunday service. For the next hour or two, both Margaret and I were miserable, envisioning that inevitable moment.

In our Christian community, it is quite normal to see numbers of parents take their children outside during meetings. (Parents are encouraged to sit near the back.) Moments later they return. It's amazing how quietly the children sit upon their return.

For those parents who wonder about little children's sitting in meetings, we definitely recommend training children to do so. (Scriptures concerning the place of little children in the congregation are numerous. A few include Joshua 8:33–35, 2 Chronicles 20:13, Luke 18:15, and Mark 10:14.) As long as meetings are not too long or too boring (in our meetings children are encouraged to clap, dance, play tambourines, and bring plastic toy instruments), little children can learn to sit quietly when necessary. Parents must train children in five- to ten-minute increments at home, gradually increasing their time. Bringing crackers to nibble, coloring books, a favorite blanket, and Bible picture books are important components as well. This was by far our most challenging task with Justin (who is a very active child), yet beginning at ten months we saw regular improvement as we remained faithful to the task.

I read last month of a study done of churches in Australia. In a search for common characteristics among the growing fellowships, one significant point was found. Those fellowships that included the children in the time of worship were growing. Those fellowships that segregated the children and had worship only for adults were stagnant or declining.

Recently Doris and I received a letter from a mother which should also prove interesting at this point:

> I would like to share with you both that in obedience to teaching in lesson eleven, to bring children to meetings and worship, we brought our son, Randy, eleven, and daughter, Tiffany, four, to lesson twelve. Tiffany sat and colored and ate raisins and very quietly sang to herself throughout your entire two-hour presentation. The next day, when asked, *she* plainly stated, "The rod brings repentance to a sinful nature." *Wow!* She remembered you taking off your "frown face" and putting on your "happy face." And she could do your whole routine on "bad attitude." While I thought she wasn't paying any attention, she was acting like a little sponge, just taking it all in. When Randy was asked to clean his room he obediently got up from the living room, *no complaints, no excuses, no change in attitude,* and went in and cleaned his room—truly a manifestation of the power of God.
>
> Really guys, keep up the *great work!*

To apply loving correction immediately, remember this last tip: Keep a number of rods throughout the house, in your car, and in your purse. Not only is it important for ready usage but it's also amazing how rods of correction can mysteriously disappear!

Out-of-Sight

This principle should be self-evident based upon all we've said thus far. Loving correction is to shape the will and modify behavior, not to humiliate or embarrass a child. For this reason, it should be done in private. (NOTE: For children under eighteen months, correction in public isn't harmful, if no private place is available.)

Neutral Object

The final element of loving correction is the instrument one uses in the process. Scripture makes it clear that it is a neutral object—"the rod of correction"—and not a belt buckle, hairbrush, or the nearest thing.

> Foolishness is bound up in the heart of a child; but the rod of correction shall drive it far from him.
>
> Proverbs 22:15 KJV

The biblical definition of the rod is a small, flexible branch from a tree (a wooden stick). Many people carve out some rods of their own or simply purchase some inexpensive wooden spoons.

Unless it is a rare emergency, we should try never to use our hands as an instrument of loving correction. The hand should be used for expressing affection and tenderness. Otherwise, our children will flinch and retreat when it is raised. Remember: A child tends to associate pain with whatever inflicts it.

Also, the very process of getting the rod and then putting it away conveys the objectivity and the finality of the correction. "Whew, it's over. Now I can start fresh!"

Pat Fabrizio, coauthor with her husband of *Children— Fun or Frenzy?* shares in her leaflet how one morning she told her little daughter to go lie across the footstool because she had disobeyed and deserved a spanking. Pat was busy in the kitchen and failed to go in immediately. When she did, there was her daughter, lying on her tummy across the footstool, waiting for her spanking, all the while singing and swinging her feet. She knew she had disobeyed, and now came the consequences via the neutral object—the rod. Once administered, it was over and she could go on with her play.

"Where is the rod administered?"

God, in His wisdom, prepared a strategic place on our children's anatomy which has enough cushiony, fatty tissue and sensitive nerve endings to respond to Spirit-led stimulation. This area is the base of the back, above the thighs, located directly on the backside of every child. All children come equipped with one!

On the lips of him who has understanding wisdom is found, but a rod is for the back of him who lacks sense.

Proverbs 10:13

> A whip for the horse, a bridle for the ass, and a rod for the back of fools.
>
> Proverbs 26:3

In loving correction, God intends us to use a neutral object—the rod. Parents will never get anywhere until they accept, in faith, the rod as God's appointed instrument of *loving*—the essential foundation, and

Clarity
Obedience
Right Attitudes
Restoration
Explanation
Consistency
Thoroughness
Immediately
Out-of-Sight
Neutral Object

Blessed is everyone who fears the Lord,
who walks in His ways!
You shall eat the fruit of the labor of your hands;
you shall be happy, and it shall be well with you.
Your wife will be like a fruitful vine within your house;
your children will be like olive shoots
around your table.
Lo, thus shall the man be blessed
who fears the Lord.
The Lord bless you from Zion!

May you see the prosperity of Jerusalem all the days of
   your life!
May you see your children's children!
Peace be upon Israel!

                                        Psalm 128

Need anything more be said?

The Bible speaks of those who are "ever learning, and
never coming into knowledge" (*see* 2 Timothy 3:7 KJV).
In other words, they are people who are ever evaluating
and considering, but never reaching any decision and
acting upon it.

We would like to close by challenging you to act now
upon what you've just read.

First, if you have never turned to God from self—by
trusting Jesus to come into your life, to forgive you your
sins and make you what He wants you to be: a joyous
child of the King—then will you be honest with Him
right now?

Jesus said that if we want to follow Him we must first
count the cost. It's not easy to do this, for we need to be
willing to let go of any habit, any plan, any person, any
activity that interferes with His marvelous design for our
lives. We must commit ourselves to radical obedience to
His Word, regardless of what our feelings or friends may
dictate. Lordship means "an end to life on my own
terms." To compromise or "sugarcoat" the cost is to
"pervert the gospel" (Galatians 1:7), and ultimately this
prevents us from learning the truth. His call is not just to
believe but to obey.

Yet if we'll look to Jesus not as some ho-hum, high,

holy and unreachable marble god who's intent on making us miserable, but rather as a friend who's "for us and not against us" (*see* Romans 8:31), then the decision is obvious. Instead of being dragged to Him kicking and screaming, we come willingly and fall into the security of His arms. Please understand that Jesus loves you and wants to be your friend as well as your Lord: one who "sticks closer than a brother" (Proverbs 18:24). He's the Good Shepherd who sees us as sheep having gone astray. He wants to put us back on the path of life. Visualize Him in this light.

Will you trust His love? Will you allow Him to rescue you from going in a way that ends in inevitable, spiritual death (frustration, misery, and confusion which comes not so much from cessation of life as from separation from the Source of life)? "There is a way which seems right to a man, but its end is the way to death" (Proverbs 14:12).

Having counted the cost, will you talk to Him while His Holy Spirit is upon you? You might say something like this:

Jesus, thanks for loving me. Thanks for demonstrating that "greater love has no man than this, that a man lay down his life for his friends" (John 15:13). Certainly You have shown Your love for me. Right now I confess that I've been selfish—doing my own thing in the kingdom of darkness. But I now repent—I turn around—and give You total control of my life. I declare an end to life on my own terms. I commit myself to obey the Word of

God and to let it be my standard throughout life. From this moment on, I take my place in the Kingdom of light and proudly proclaim You, Jesus, as Lord of my life.

If this prayer expresses the desire of your heart, pray it now. You will become a new creation (2 Corinthians 5:17), enter a new Kingdom, and start out on a new path of life. Regardless of how dark and gloomy the future looks for the unrighteous of this world, you can move forward with quiet confidence undergirded by the promises of the Word of God. "But the path of the righteous is like the light of dawn, which shines brighter and brighter until full day" (Proverbs 4:18).

Second, in your biblical responsibility as a parent, will you join with me and scores of other followers of Jesus Christ in committing yourself to loving correction of your children?

Will you commit yourself to settle for nothing but the best in terms of what God has intended for your family?

Jesus desires to smash the meaningless and worldly counterfeits by raising up end-time Christian homes to be a model of His better way.

Will you accept the challenge?

Review

1. What do the letters in the acrostic C.O.R.R.E.C.
   T.I.O.N. stand for? Explain each one.
2. Why might it be important to commit this to memory?
3. Explain the statement "Spanking is an event."

4. What are the two main areas we as parents need to work on with our children? Explain.

5. Explain the significance of "restoration" in loving correction.

6. Why is the hand not effective in loving correction?

7. What prevents us from being consistent? What can we do to overcome such hindrances?

Response

Did I respond to my loving Creator by committing myself to loving correction of my children?

Suggested Reading

Adams, Jay. *Competent to Counsel.* Grand Rapids, Mich.: Baker Book House, 1979.

Campbell, Dr. Ross. *How to Really Love Your Child.* Wheaton, Ill.: Victor Books, 1977.

Christenson, Larry. *The Christian Family.* Minneapolis, Minn.: Bethany Fellowship, Inc., 1970.

Dobson, James. *The Strong-Willed Child.* Wheaton, Ill.: Tyndale House Pubs., 1978.

Fabrizio, Al, and Fabrizio, Pat. *Children—Fun or Frenzy?* Algeria Press, 1969.

Lessin, Roy. *How to Be Parents of Happy, Obedient Children.* Van Nuys, Calif.: Bible Voice, Inc., 1978.

MacDonald, Gordon. *The Effective Father.* Wheaton, Ill.: Tyndale House Pubs., 1977.

Taylor, Richard S. *The Disciplined Life.* Minneapolis, Minn.: Bethany Fellowship, Inc., 1974.